THE RESURRECTION OF
ROMANCE

How to Create And Sustain
A World-Class Romantic Relationship
That Lasts A Lifetime !

BY

MATTHEW ANDERSON D.MIN.

INTERNATIONAL
#1 BEST
SELLER

THE RESURRECTION OF
ROMANCE

Romantic love, Ecstasy and Radical Intimacy

*How to create a world class
romantic relationship
that lasts a lifetime!*

MATTHEW ANDERSON, D.MIN.

*Romantic love is not meant to die.
It is meant to flower and blossom
for as long as the two of you
sustain and nurture it.*

To Bev & Lawrence,

May your path together
be filled with love!

Matthew
2018

DEDICATION

To my Love and my Sunshine

who is my muse

and my greatest inspiration for this book.

*Many
easy-to-read
brief chapters!*

Enjoy!

ACKNOWLEDGMENTS

I offer my deep and heartfelt thanks to Jason Chanowski for his support, and enthusiasm and especially for the wonderful creation and design of our blog www.TheResurrectionofRomance.com .

A special thanks also to Steve Saley of Leverage2 for the beautiful and stunning design of the book cover.

Hugs and thanks to Heidi Moss, also of Leverage2, for her support and expert help with social media and her consistent encouragement.

Thanks to John Ireland for his expertise and persistence in getting this book to the public.

Thank you to all the couples who have shared their love and their difficulties with me for over 40 years. You have been superb teachers. God bless you all.

Finally, thank you to Dianna and Michael. Without you there would be no resurrection of romance!

INTRODUCTION

Science has given us innumerable breakthroughs in our understanding of the material world that have led to innovations that were beyond our imagination. Now romantic love in the context of radical intimacy offers couples a similar opportunity to walk through its doorway into a new world of long term romantic relationship filled with ecstasy, joy, growth and healing.

Why is this possible? It began with the new equality of women. Radical intimacy is only possible with a peer and now both women and men are dramatically changing their beliefs, attitudes and perceptions about the value, power and equality of women.

The deepest possibilities of intimacy and love disappear when one partner is seen as superior or inferior to the other. Imbalance on either side generates a power disparity and that disparity creates fear, and fear always blocks the flow of intimacy. Fear causes hiding and hiding and intimacy are opposites. The more we hide the less we can share openly with our partner, and intimacy depends on unfettered openness.

Never before in recorded history and possibly since the dawn of human beings, has the equality of women been a true possibility. Historically, every major religion and most, if not all, cultures have fostered inequality between men and women, and it is only in recent decades that this belief has begun to erode.

Now, since the mid-twentieth century, women are beginning to be seen (by themselves and by men) as peers with men. Thus radical intimacy is becoming a reality in an increasing number of couples. It is radical intimacy that provides the nurturing energy and depth that sustains the wonder and ecstasy of romantic love. However, without its very specific care and sustenance, romantic love dissipates and finally disappears.

Romantic love has the power to open the door and set the stage for radical intimacy. It breaks into our lives without warning and takes over every aspect of our existence. This power, in truth, is numinous (divine) and it cannot be resisted. Suddenly our hearts and souls drop their walls and we, hand in loving hand with our partner, enter a world of naked vulnerability in which we are seen and see in what could best be called a holy light. It is here that we come to see the best of who we (and our partner) are and can be.

We call this experience "falling in love" because of its joyful, helpless quality. We are unable to stop the feelings, thoughts and behaviors that it generates. We find ourselves radically exposed to the one who has become our Beloved and they to us. It can bring deep healing and a transformation of our sense of self and our possibilities that is more wonderful than anything we have ever experienced. Yet, sadly, even tragically, it usually ends in months and we are left confused, disappointed and with an expectation that it will never appear again.

The loss of romantic love is so common that almost every couple expects it to disappear, and it is that very expectation combined with lack of intimacy skills and a real sense of equality between partners that make that loss a reality. The good news is that this need not occur. The best news is that, under the right circumstances, with the right expectations and skills, radical intimacy can flourish and romantic love can continue to blossom without limit.

Romantic love creates a portal to ecstasy, rapture, bliss, joy and passion. Our task as lovers is not to stand at the doorway and peer through into the beauties beyond. Yes, the vision before us is astounding and exhilarating and we can be enthralled by what we see for months but simply looking will not sustain our ecstasy. To stand and look passively at the glory that romantic love offers us is the quickest way to slam the door shut. Doorways are created for action not observation. Romantic love shows up and suddenly where there was only a dark and empty space there is now an opening into a magnificent, glowing world of re- lationship like no other we have ever imagined. If we allow ourselves to become mesmerized by the sight and do not accept the simultaneous call to action, we will miss the transforming miracle it offers. The door will swing shut and we will find ourselves with only a memory and a closed door. This is what happens to the great majority of lovers and it is a sad and tragic end to what could have been the beginning of the most joy filled journey of their lives.

Too often couples think of romantic love like a hot bath. It feels won- derfully blissful at first and they bask in its warmth. And then, day by day it begins to cool until their relationship assumes a lukewarm quality. They remain completely unaware that they could stoke the fire and sustain the blissful warmth and they accept the loss as the nature of love. Once it loses its intensity they either live in the tepid waters of an insipid relationship or leave the bath and go in search of another lover and the hope of finding the new heat of love.

The difficulty is in the popular but toxic assumption that romantic love has a limited life-span which cannot be extended. This perception will always lead, at best, to mediocre relationships and at worst to separation or divorce. There is, however, another way to see romantic love and that is as a call to action. It must be viewed as an invitation to walk through a doorway into a world where love is allowed and encouraged to grow and expand without the loss of bliss and joy and ecstasy, a world in which both lovers find the highest and best in each other and in themselves.

Imagine sailing, lost for weeks on a seemingly endless sea and finally you see land ahead. You anchor off an unexplored coast and swim ashore. You are so happy to find dry land that you kneel and kiss the beach.

Then you do something that might appear strange or even insane.

You set up camp on that beach and end your journey. You never walk inland to discover the wonders of the new country you have discovered. You live your life as a beachcomber, unwilling or unable to travel into the vast and mysterious land that begins just feet from where you came ashore. Eventually that beach, once so beautiful to your sea-weary eyes, becomes tiny and confining, even boring, and you begin to have fantasies of setting out to sea again.

This brief tale is the story of almost all lovers. They fall in love and find a wonderful new country together. Then they stagnate and never get off the beach and finally all their joy, bliss and exhilaration disappear. They never explore the new country that has been offered to them. Why? Why do so many of us stop there and never go further. It is because we do not have a map and a guide and maybe we are afraid and maybe we have been told that the beach is all there is and to expect more is to be foolish. The truth is, the land of romantic love is more vast and beautiful than we could imagine and it promises great treasures to any couple willing to venture off the beach.

A Personal Note

I grew up in the Deep South in a family of devout evangelical Christians. Both the culture and the religion held women as inferior to men. Yet an unpredictable complexity of events and relationships protected me from the pervasive negative perception of women. My grandmother (Nanny) on my mother's side was like a second mother to me and I spent many hundreds of hours in her home observing her relationship with Granddaddy. He had just retired when I was born and she, being 10 years younger, was still working. Nanny was the Director and main teacher of the local kindergarten and as her grandson I was allowed to enter a year early. I spent 2 years under her tutelage and always viewed her as an authority who was wise, loving and capable. At home, Granddaddy was a quiet and somewhat formal gentleman who never fought with her (at least in my presence). He always treated her with respect and I never once heard him say a negative word about her. Nanny did not retire until I was around 15 and thus I always experienced her as a professional person who was a consistent bread winner.

My mother was very close to Nanny and emulated her in many ways. She also worked (in a bank) and married a man who respected her, never spoke ill of her and, at least from my growing up viewpoint, treated her and my grandmother with complete respect. And, like Nanny and Granddaddy, my parents never fought in my presence. The lack of verbal conflict in both relationships protected me from hearing and internalizing the inevitable nasty, hurtful, put-downs that couples often say in the midst of a fight. I never heard my father or grandfather say even one sexist remark about their wives or other women. I cannot say this was because they were so wonderfully liberated in their consciousness. They were not. They both held true many of the prejudices of their time but did not voice these attitudes to me and thus I was not infected by them.

I grew up respecting my mother and women in general but was not really aware that I lacked an attitude of male superiority until I was in my twenties which coincided with the sixties. I was 15 in 1960 and took easily to the new attitudes about freedom and equality, especially as they applied to women. Eventually, I married a woman with two daughters and we had a daughter together and women's rights and women as equals were the order of the day for me. I saw women as peers then and I still do. These special circumstances and attitudes made it possible for me to approach radical intimacy with the appropriate stance and context for me and my partner.

As a Coach/counselor over the last 4 decades, I have worked with hundreds of couples who were having relationship difficulties. In almost every case, intimacy has been an issue and the lack of a true sense of equality has been one of the central contributing factors in their discord. We will discuss this issue at length including how each partner can make meaningful changes to create a peer relationship with her or his partner in the following pages.

How I came to value intimacy and romantic love so strongly is a bit more mysterious. I was born an empath. This means that I had/have an unusual ability to sense and feel other people's emotions. By the time I reached my late teens I realized that I also valued deep and meaningful relationships and had little interest in shallow and superficial communication. Both values set me on a path to become a helping professional (counselor/coach) whose work both requires and enhances both values. This book is a testimony to my family and their contributions to my appreciation and understanding of equality in relationships and ultimately to the value or radical intimacy and romantic love.

Matthew Anderson

December, 2015

Five Toxic Myths about Romantic Love

Each of the myths listed below is commonly held in our culture and each has had a negative (toxic) effect on the power and sustainability of romantic love. Each one needs to be challenged and changed if romantic love is to be resurrected. Each myth, therefore, is followed by a truth that offers hope and new possibilities for all romantically involved couples. Each of these myths and their corresponding truths are explored in detail in the following chapters.

Myth: Romantic love has to end sooner than later and certainly cannot be sustained for years or decades.

Truth: Romantic love does not have to end and can be respected, sustained, nurtured, and expanded and deepened.

Myth: Romantic love is a form of intoxication (i.e. a form of poison/pathology).

Truth: Romantic love is actually a form of ecstasy and is the antidote to poison – a detox of the highest order.

Myth: Romantic love causes a loss of self.

Truth: Romantic love is a loss of the little self (ego) in the service of the Greater Self (Atman).

Myth: Romantic love creates an unrealistic ("romantic") view of the other.

Truth: Romantic love gives us the Eyes of Love which help us see the real Beauty of and in the Beloved.

Myth: Marriage ends romantic love.

Truth: Conscious marriage based on radical intimacy nurtures and grows romantic love and ecstasy.

CHAPTER 1

Dianna and Michael – An Explanation

Both Dianna and Michael have expressed a concern from the beginning of their sharing for this book. They wonder if some readers might think their relationship is too sweet or perfect. Here is their conversation about that issue. Dianna asked to begin.

"Honey, I sometimes worry that people who read this and hear about how we are together might think we are too sappy, too sweet and they might actually get nauseous when they see how we relate. My second fear is that they could imagine that we are not telling the whole truth and only share the good stuff. I think both my concerns need to be addressed so that everyone who reads this will understand that we are not faking this and that we are not hiding anything important or negative about who we are as a couple."

Michael nods emphatically and picks up the conversation.

"I agree 100%! We are definitely unusual and our relationship is far from normal. And yes, some people might think we are too tender and careful and sappy as you say. I also think we should speak clearly to the idea that we might be hiding the dark side of our relationship. So I want to say a couple of things and then you can add to it and we can go from there. (Dianna nods a yes)

"I have observed hundreds of couples over the years and have been in relationship myself and the truth is, ours is exceptional. In fact it may be the best I have ever known or even heard of. I am not bragging here. We both came to this relationship with different but difficult histories. We both suffered, some by our own hands and some by the hands of our partners. We have been determined to learn from our mistakes and the mistakes of our past relationships. I mean truly determined. We make an enormous effort every single day to nurture and grow our love together. We think deeply about who we are as a couple and we talk a lot about what works for us and what would create problems. We are both particularly careful to be adult and loving whenever any tension arises. We definitely hold our love as incredibly precious and we are fiercely determined to protect it from anything and anyone who might pose a threat to it.

"Yes, we are a bit sappy and sweet with each other but that is real stuff. It is not an act. You are my Sweetheart and my Honey and my Dear and I am all that and more to you. Yes, I love you so much that I hate it if I upset you even for a moment. Your well being is more important to me than my ego and that simple but significant fact really makes a difference in how we relate. You are exactly the same and between us we seem to always remember that when the crap hits the fan, and it does for us as much as in any normal relationship. Our lives are not free from any of the normal stresses that other couples face. Not at all. But when it shows up we pull together rather than allow it to pull us apart. We might look or sometimes sound too dear with each other but that care is real and very strong and woe to anyone who tries to mess with it."

Dianna laughs warmly at Michael's last comment and begins to speak again.

"Honey, I love it when you get passionate about us. And you are right. We are generally tender and sweet with each other. It is good for the care and feeding of our romance. And yes, we do have stresses that we deal with regularly. But when stress occurs we both refuse to allow our dark sides to participate in the conversation. We don't attack each other. We don't curse each other. We don't play childish games and we especially don't jump on the other when mistakes are made. When tension begins to show up we both try really hard to be more patient and understanding and we surely don't hold grudges. In fact, every time we handle a situation that could have erupted in a nasty fight with other partners, I think we become a bit proud of ourselves that we are doing this in a new and wonderful way."

Michael strongly agrees with this!

"Honey, you are so right. We have many opportunities to cross the line and fall into hurtful interaction. Life has no shortage of those for us. But that is where our commitment makes the difference. We want this to work and we are willing to find whatever level of maturity and compassion and understanding it takes to get through it with respect and care for this precious thing we share.

"I hope that whoever reads this trusts that we are for real. If they do then they might find some new hope for themselves and their relationship. I know you agree with me, Honey. It is why we are sharing so openly about what we have together."

Chapter 2

Falling in Love is not a Choice

Falling in love is never a choice. We have no control over its appearance and it's incredibly powerful grasp on our hearts and bodies and minds. One moment we are in charge and the next moment love runs the show. This is why we use the phrase falling in love because it is so accurate. No one wakes up one morning and decides that today will be the day to fall in love. It happens to us, rather than us happening to it. It is the way of love and especially romantic love.

Romantic love, the ecstatic, head-over-heels, heart bursting experience of love for another person, shows up on its own mysterious time table. It cannot be predicted or manipulated, nor does it respect any of the normal boundaries of culture, tradition, religion, race or age. It decides when and where and with whom and woe to one who, for any reason, resists its charms or tries to come between lovers.

For all its wonderful blessings and joy, romantic love can sometimes create confusion and conflict when it grasps the hearts of two unsuspecting individuals whose lives may not be prepared for the changes it demands. The chosen lovers may be of different cultures or social status; they may be far apart in age or physical local; they may be committed to celibacy or even married to someone else. Love seems not to care about any of these complications. It has its own logic and timing and, try as we may, we cannot change it even in a small way. Our only choices are to resist or surrender.

Resisting romantic love can cause serious crisis in a life. Our responses may be ethical or utilitarian but whether supported by morality or convenience, they seldom change the convictions of the heart. Once true love fills us from head to toe we would be love-wise to surrender. Then, once surrendered, we will become its servant and will be strengthened and guided by its particular and inspired direction.

Our American culture is obsessed with the idea of choice. We demand choices in everything from ice cream to bottled water to real estate and vocation and when it comes to love we expect the same freedom. But love is beyond our control and rarely cooperates with our sense of entitlement. When it appears we are so enthralled with our connection to our beloved that we often forget that we did not choose this person. Somehow, in accordance with some mysterious and miraculous plan, we fall into a love-trap set specifically for us. Our only real choice is to resist and suffer or surrender and allow love to become our guide.

Chapter 3

Dianna and Michael – Love is not a Choice

Dianna gives Michael a playful dig in his ribs and tells him to begin the conversation.

"OK, I know you think I have lots of opinions about this one. You are right, Honey, and I always like it when you are right. (He smiles) So here goes. I am completely convinced that romantic love, falling in love with someone, the head-over-heels variety, is no more a choice for us human beings, than our skin color. When it comes to this sort of love we are powerless. In fact, powerlessness is a basic part of the deal. This sort of powerlessness is a form of freedom. We don't have to think about it, measure it, analyze it or make a stupid pros and cons list. It is and we are and that is that. Done deal. That gives us the opportunity to drop out of the power game and allow our hearts to drive the bus. Once we do that, the ride is pretty incredible. It has been for us and I think it is for lots of other couples who surrender to love. What do you think, Sweetheart?"

Dianna pauses to clear her thoughts and shares.

"Honey, just to make a brief aside, I love it that you really do like it when I am right. I know you are not joking about that and that is so great. OK, now about falling in love. Yes, it really is not a choice. When I fell for you, it was nothing like choosing a TV set or anything else that involves options. It was BANG! And BOOM! And you were so far into my heart I could not imagine ever getting you out even if I wanted to and I have never wanted that even for a moment.

"I do know what you mean about surrender but the feeling I have is not what I imagined surrender would be like. I always thought of surrender as a kind of giving up, like in war. But this is not war, this is love and it is another form of surrender. It is sweet and easy and tender and sort of like easing down into a hot bubble bath at the end of a hard day. Loving you is so good for me, I would be crazy to resist it. And, Honey, I think you feel the same way. Could you say a little more about this idea of powerlessness? I think that is important."

Michael agrees and continues.

"Powerlessness can be very scary to many people. We tend to think it means being out of control like trying to drive a car that suddenly loses its brakes. But it is not like that. The powerlessness of romantic love is a good thing. It means that we can let go and enjoy the ride because love is at the wheel. Yes, it does involve some trust but trusting in love is what this is all about. Once love shows up, I think the best thing to do is to let go and let it drive the bus."

Chapter 4

Intoxication vs Ecstasy

Romantic love is not a drug that makes us exhilarated and then drops us to the hard ground without mercy. It is not like speed or cocaine or LSD or any narcotic and is especially unlike alcohol. Romantic love does not cause intoxication and to think of it this way is to completely miss its real ecstatic possibilities. To be intoxicated literally means to be infused with a poison. A poison is by definition something that is extremely harmful and even deadly. Intoxication disconnects us from our best self. It shuts off our awareness and blocks our access to higher levels of feeling and thinking. It blunts our sensitivity, blinds our ability to see ourselves or others clearly and ultimately makes us deaf and dumb to love. Intoxication is actually the complete opposite of the ecstasy of romantic love and we do not need to de-tox from what is truly ecstatic.

For centuries many writers, poets and recently, relationship professionals have confused intoxication with the ecstasy of romantic love and by doing so have caused great damage to the understanding of an experience that is the true opposite of becoming drunk on a poisonous substance. Any substance, material or emotional, that intoxicates ultimately causes its host to shrink, dissipate and die. On the other hand, ecstasy, the kind that graces romantic love, brings the best that life has to offer. If intoxication blunts sensitivity, ecstasy enhances it. If intoxication shrinks, ecstasy expands. If intoxication takes us down into the nether regions of our worst and most degraded selves then ecstasy draws us up to mountains top experiences where we are gifted with the sight to see all the beauty of creation.

To confuse ecstasy with intoxication will lead us to the quick end of romantic love because in expecting it to eventually wear itself out, as do all drunken binges, we will not learn the attitudes, behaviors and special skills that nurture and sustain it. Then we will stand helpless before its dwindling and weep at its passing, become maudlin in our memory of it and sing sad songs about lovers who began with a burst of feeling and ended in decades of insipid coupling.

If, however, we walk together through the doorway provide by romantic love, we can expect a continued experience of ecstasy and all the special grace-filled gifts that it brings. One of the most life changing is what I have come to call the Eyes of Love (see Chapter 25).

Chapter 5

Dianna and Michael – Intoxication vs. Ecstasy

Dianna speaks first.

"Let me go first Sweetheart. I love this topic. I never felt ecstasy before I fell in love with you. I did drugs in college and some of them were pretty intense, and I felt feelings I had never imagined when I gave birth to three dear children but this, falling in love with you, this has been more than I thought I could handle. I feel sometimes as if my insides are going to explode with love. I shake and I tremble and when we make love, well you know what I mean, I burst out in tears and they feel so sweetly tender and my heart swells and it seems like it is pouring love through my eyes. Honey, being with you that way, it is better than anything I have known and I could live on it forever with you."

Dianna's eyes fill with tears and she takes Michael's face in her hands and kisses him over and over and he smiles and hugs her and then he continues the conversation.

"Yes, Sweetheart, I feel exactly the way you do. And I hate to hear anyone talk about this thing and call it being intoxicated. That is what college kids do on a weekend. They drink themselves silly and act even sillier and then black out and don't even remember what happened. That is being intoxicated. To call what we experience intoxicated is just plain stupid. We don't forget. In fact, we remember almost every single precious detail and we love to share those memories with each other. It is almost like living it all over again. And we don't have ecstasy hangovers either. We feel better, not worse, after being high that way together. We like ourselves better. We appreciate what we have and we get high on feeling grateful for it. That is nothing like being drunk. Nothing."

Diana, touches his arm in support.

"Honey, let it go. I know that upsets you when people talk that way about what we know is sacred and special and so precious to us. It only means they have never been there. They have no idea. It is too bad for them."

Michael relents and continues.

"Thanks, honey. I get really pissed about this. But the fact is, you are right! Most people like that put down what they don't know and then they miss out on the best thing that could ever happen to them. But something that bothers me even more is that so many couples fall in love and really experience this ecstasy and it is so beautiful for them and then they screw around with it and neglect it and it dies and they end up accepting an incredibly mundane, mediocre, greyed-out existence as a couple, and they decide that is normal and how it is supposed to be.

That really sucks! I never want to be that way. Never! I promise you I will do everything I can to make sure we hold on to this beautiful thing we have, Honey. I promise with every cell in this body!"

Dianna smiles and takes his hand.

"Michael, I love you so much when you get this passionate. You make my heart so happy. I think I want to make love with you right now."

They both laugh and hug.

Chapter 6

Life inside the Palace

When we are "in love" we feel completed, as though a missing part of ourselves had been returned to us; we feel uplifted, as though we were suddenly raised above the level of the ordinary world. Life has an intensity, a glory, an ecstasy and transcendence. Robert Johnson

What occurs once two lovers walk through the entryway of the Palace of Romantic Love and into the deeper and more mysterious rooms of the Palace?

It is both impossible and inappropriate to attempt to describe this experience without using quite a lot of romantic and poetic language because it is the only language spoken within these sacred walls. Romantic love always seems to empower the heart to speak this way and couples who venture deeper become increasingly fluent in it. Each couple will have their own special twist to their intimate and loving communication but the essential language remains no matter their age, race, culture or education. To those who remain in the shadowy forest outside the Palace, it can sound quaint, corny, mushy and even too sweet, but to the initiated it is a language of powerful joy and ecstatic love.

Chapter 7

Dianna and Michael – Life inside the Palace

In their eagerness to share, they both begin to speak at once, and then laugh, defer to the other, and then they laugh again, and finally Dianna speaks. She is beaming and her words tumble out.

"I have to say that this experience, this love, is not like anything I ever imagined or expected or even felt I deserved. (Michael immediately nods his head in agreement.)

"I love him with every cell of my body and it seems that he feels exactly the same about me. There is no imbalance of one of us loving the other more. It flows and builds and even though at the start I thought it could not get any greater or stronger, it did. It really did and our love today is far more powerful than it was the first year and I hope and expect this will continue to grow but even if it stays exactly the same as it is now for the rest of our lives together I will feel totally and completely satisfied with what we have. (Again, Michael nods enthusiastically in smiling agreement.) I could talk forever about this but I want Michael to share. He speaks so beautifully about love and every time he talks about it I get more excited about him and our relationship. Honey, will you talk now?"

Michael becomes still for a moment and he looks into her eyes. His body relaxes and an almost imperceptible energy passes between them. It seems as if he is being filled from the inside and then he sighs and begins to speak.

"One of the most powerful and life-giving gifts of this kind of love is the ability to look at each other in the most ordinary circumstances and be immediately filled with an overwhelming burst of gratefulness for that person's presence in our lives. I often feel so touched that tears flow and I love that feeling of looking at her and seeing her beauty, her essence, not just her body, and the moment becomes sacred and she is so precious to me and I want to hold her forever. And what is so mercifully amazing is that in these moments I can tell that she feels exactly the same and that awareness takes us both over the top into what can only be described as ecstasy. (Dianna is nodding her head and smiling and mouthing the words "see I told you so, he is so wonderful!) Michael continues:

"When our relationship began we both loved the feelings and the intensity and the closeness. We both also had the expectation that this level of romance and intimacy and joy at being together would eventually dissipate. But a year passed and the opposite occurred. It got stronger and even more intense and we loved more deeply and with more tenderness and were often so grateful we cried together about it. Then two years passed and three and the same things were happening and I began to look more closely at what we might be doing to sustain and grow this very special glorious experience of love."

Michael turns to Dianna and takes her hand and extends her arm so that he can touch the inside of her elbow. He kisses her there very briefly and then begins to speak again:

"I wrote a poem about this part of her arm. Let me share it with you."

"There must be a name for the inside of an elbow.

That crease between upper and lower arm.
But I don't want to know it.
To assign a technical term for that precious and sacred space would be wrong
It would diminish the feeling that occurs
When I kiss that special dearly sweet place on her body.

I hold her arm tenderly and open it straight out as if opening her legs.
I put my lips carefully,
Ever so softly on that sweet space
My heart begins to sing.
I flutter and then pound inside and I kiss three times.
I raise my eyes to meet her dancing browns
She smiles and butter flows warmly between us.
It lubricates the connection and smile becomes embrace,
I kiss her arm again, three times and then another smile and butter
and heat rise between us
Every cell of flesh vibrates love and lust marry and call for a child to be
created out of this union.

We answer without hesitation
Now a new being emerges,
Thou, us, we
And then one, one, one.
There must be a name
But now we have moved beyond words and have no need of it."

Dianna is crying when Michael finishes reading the poem. Then she begins to share again.

"These are always beautiful moments between us. This is a moment when one of us completely opens his or her heart and allows something precious and so vulnerable to emerge. It must be received as it is sent, with the same openheartedness. Anything less will stop the flow and therefore it becomes a partnership. He gives and I receive and I give and he does the same for me and in many ways it is like making love in the best sense of that phrase. It can happen, of course, in bed, but it can also happen, and frequently does, in the most ordinary situation, like washing dishes together, or walking the dog and sometimes even in a text.

"I think this is one of the most central reasons we have sustained our intensity of romantic love for so many years. We value this kind of communication and we want to experience it daily. In fact, it is not unusual for it to occur three or four times a day on a good day and at least once on an 'off" day. "

Dianna smiles and looks at Michael when she says the work "off". Then she continues:

"I don't write poetry. That is a gift Michael brings to our relationship but as he loves to say to me, every gift of art is not complete until it is received by an art lover. I am his art-lover. I open my heart to his very special word creations and allow them to penetrate as deeply in me as the place within him that they have originated from. He can sense that and it makes him want to share more and that becomes a wonderful back and forth between us that often reaches ecstasy."

When she stops talking, Michael touches Dianna's hand and joins the conversation.

"The truth is, one does not have to be a poet to reach and sustain the level of romantic love we have together. Great poetry is as close as a book or a computer. It does not have to be original to be a powerful contributor to the connection between two lovers. The issue is whether both lovers are willing and able to open their hearts and tolerate the intensity of the connection they create. We can talk more about this later but it is crucial to the experience of romantic love. Without this special level of intimacy, romantic love loses its hold on the couple and they drift back into the mundane and eventually the wonderful ecstasy they shared is just a lovely memory. Dianna and I do everything we can to prevent that. What we have is worth every effort and the good news is that it gets easier and easier to create and sustain a wonderful level of romantic love as the years pass, not harder as most couples think."

Chapter 8

The Demands and Expectations of Romantic Love

Author and Jungian scholar, Robert A. Johnson, makes a powerful and insightful statement about the demands of romantic love in his book WE.

"This is why men and women put such impossible demands on each other in their relationships. We actually believe unconsciously that this mortal human being has the responsibility for making our lives whole, keeping us happy, making our lives meaningful, intense and ecstatic!"

Tragically, most people who fall in love eventually commit the exact mistake that Mr. Johnson describes so accurately above. Lovers become enthralled with each other and then too often lay the responsibility for the sustenance of their precious love at the feet of the other. Then, it inevitably fails. It fails because both are confused and misdirected about the real source of their love and unaware of what it really takes to sustain it. What began as blessing slowly erodes into blame. Each lover imagines that romantic ecstasy would return if their partner would only...If you would only smile more, dance better, talk more sweetly, take out the trash daily, make more money, lose 20 pounds...the list, once begun, becomes endless and leads to a dark valley of disappointment and disillusionment. Romance is lost and it is the fault of the other. Done.

It is true that we will be disappointed if we make another person responsible for our happiness and wholeness. No one can create those for us, even that dear and exquisite individual we love so much. That is a burden she or he cannot carry while we walk, unburdened and irresponsible, by their side. This selfish, immature and ill informed attitude always leads to blame and manipulation. It never ever leads back to the wonder and ecstasy that was so intense at the beginning.

The solution to the difficulty described so aptly by Mr. Johnson has two parts. First it is necessary for each partner to fully accept responsibility for his or her part in sustaining the passion of romantic love. Second, both lovers must commit to a daily practice of the attitudes and behaviors (see below) that sustain it. It is important for both to remember that romantic love came to them as an incredible gift and once it arrives it is up to them to nurture it. As stated in an earlier section, romantic love is not a choice. Its arrival is completely out of our control and in some sense it may be considered a divine gift given its astounding power to change lives. The fact that it is a holy gift is even more reason to accept it gracefully, not take it for granted, and honor it with a full commitment to its care.

Chapter 9

Dianna and Michael - Expectations

Dianna steps forward and begins the conversation.

"Honey, I suppose I would say that this very wonderful romantic thing we have together is both a blessing and a responsibility. I never met anyone who is as good at it as you are. You know I think that. But I would never expect you to be completely responsible for sustaining it. I know it is something we do together and I think we do it equally. It cannot be 80/20 or something so unbalanced like that. It needs to be 50/50. We both have to do our part. What do you think?"

Michael has great energy about this topic and he starts talking immediately.

"Sweetheart, I agree with you but I want to change the numbers a bit. I know this might sound strange at first but, in truth, I think it actually describes how we do it, and how I think all couples should approach it. I think each partner should take 100% responsibility for the care and nurturing of their romantic relationship! I know this does not make mathematical sense but it makes love sense. Here is how I came to this conclusion and these numbers.

"If we do 50/50 we still expect the other person to do their part. Expectation then becomes part of the process and it is easy to keep score. One person begins to think they are doing more and even if it is a few percentage points, they begin to build resentment. I think we should both take 100% responsibility. That way, I do not expect anything from you. I am always focused on what I need to do to make this relationship happy and healthy. I don't have any energy to watch or evaluate you or your contribution. And, yes, some people might think that would make it easy to take advantage of me and shirk any contribution or responsibility. But, in fact, it actually makes the other person grateful and eager to contribute fully. When you see me give with all my heart to you and our love, you feel inspired to do the same. It is a matter of trust and real giving of our love, and it really works. When one person gives 100% and the other does the same without expectation or obligation, it creates something akin to 200% and that, my Love, is why our relationship is so astounding. Am I making sense here, Honey?"

Dianna smiles and responds.

"Sweetheart, you did it again. I love this idea! Yes, I do think we both give 100% and we never get into any conflict about who is not contributing. In fact, we both frequently remark about how much the other person gives. In all the time we have been together I don't think I once thought that you were not doing everything you could to care for our romance. I think you feel the same about me and I want to keep it that way."

Michael nods in agreement and adds to the conversation.

"Honey, thanks! I have always felt you were great at this and I want to give back as much as you give to me. That is where this idea of 100% from both partners came from. I never want to fall into that trap in which I am watching how much you give. I love you and I am here 100%. That makes me free from blaming and judging and I would hate it if we became that way. My goal is to create the best romance ever with you. I think we both do a super job of that!"

Chapter 10

What is Radical Intimacy? – A New Definition

The word radical literally means going to the root or source of something. In the context of a romantic relationship, radical intimacy means giving one's Beloved total access to one's inner being (source, root) in a continuing act of loving self-revelation and sacrifice and simultaneously receiving the inner being (source, root) of one's Beloved as a precious and sacred gift.

Total access to one's inner being does not mean that we necessarily communicate every thought, feeling or memory that exists in our minds. It does mean that we sacrifice gladly our ego defenses and allow our partner to see who we really were, are and hope to be. This process can be frightening and extremely difficult if it is attempted outside the context of romantic love. But romantic love creates a very special atmosphere in which we can find the courage and ability to bare our souls with our Beloved, and in that process find a new and glorious vision of self and the other.

Radical intimacy, in the hands of romantic love, becomes a process that shapes our daily interaction with our Beloved. It introduces us to a preciously rare level of non-defensive vulnerability that allows a heart-to-heart flow of communication of words, touch, seeing and being seen and emotion that is almost completely unavailable to the non-initiated. Here, two lovers enter a world of closeness and intense sensitivity that transcends normal relationship. They slip easily past the boundaries and blunders of immaturity, defensiveness, sarcasm, hurt, anger and misunderstanding into a space of tenderness, gentleness, gratefulness and joy. Conflict becomes almost non-existent and in its place emerges an ever growing experience of grace and preciousness that permeates every interaction.

Radical intimacy produces a non-ordinary experience of relationship. It is so unusual that even its joy becomes difficult to tolerate and most couples will, after they have reached their toleration point, begin to unconsciously generate behavior that erodes it. This can occur in various ways but immaturity usually provides the most effective intimacy-blocking behavior. Couples at this stage will say hurtful childish things, become irritated by relatively insignificant habits or comments, add sarcasm to humor, offer criticism at inopportune moments and embarrass each other in public. The list immaturity generated negativity is endless but the effects are immediate, and the doorway to deep closeness begins to shut. In weeks the thrill disappears and a new status quo of livable distance is established. Sadly, it is in this state that the majority of committed relationships live out their existence. Romance and the special connection it created are gone and a new sort of toleration takes root and the myth, that romantic love cannot endure, rules.

The problem, contrary to popular opinion, even including those professionals that should know better, is not with romantic love and its inherent inability to last. The almost inevitable loss of the wonder and ecstasy of romantic love is due to four heretofore unacknowledged factors: Our inability to tolerate ecstasy and joy, partner inequality, immaturity, and lack of radical intimacy skills. The good news is that each of these potentially destructive factors can be attended to so that a couple can rediscover or resurrect their experience of romantic love and allow it to become the defining context for their relationship.

Chapter 11

Dianna and Michael – Radical Intimacy

What are your thoughts about radical intimacy and romantic love?

Michael is eager to speak about this subject and he quickly offers a meaningful response.

"It is my experience that romantic love comes suddenly, like a lightning bolt out of a clear sky. It strikes and tears open a window in two hearts and something both grace-filled and divine begins to flow between the two. The great Sufi master Shams I Tabriz once quoted a line from the Koran which says *'From heart to heart there is a window'*. I am convinced that there is a window in every heart, yes, but few allow light to shine out of and into it. Romantic love, when it strikes, makes that possible, at least for a while, but then the two lovers must do their part in sustaining that light and its flow. That is the point at which what we call radical intimacy is essential."

Dianna is enthusiastic about this subject and enters the conversation.

"I agree with all of this. We fell in love at first sight or at least very close to that. The feelings for me were so strong they were almost scary at first. (She laughs) But I got past the fear very quickly and I was actually the one who said 'I love you' first. I remember the day and the place and the moment and I also remember that I did not plan to say it. The words simply appeared in my mouth and I looked at Michael and said them and wow it was wonderful. I also remember that he did not say 'I love you' back at that point. He looked in my eyes and hugged me and that was fine. He waited a couple of days and told me he loved me too and that he had waited to make sure I knew he was not pressured into it by my sharing.

"We immediately went to a deeper level in our relationship once we talked about love. Our sharing got more personal, of course, and we began to have many intimate encounters. I am not talking about sex or lovemaking here. That is another very amazing and special conversation all by itself. I mean really, really intimate. I mean face to face, heart to heart, sharing that often felt to me that we were completely naked even when we had all our clothes on. It was and still is a very, very powerful experience that can only be called ecstatic. It could last a moment or much longer. It is hard to judge the time when we are so connected. There have actually been times when we stayed that way for hours even if we were out in public shopping or at the beach or taking a drive. I think we both were surprised at the intensity but we both love it and we talk a lot about what happens between us and how beautiful it is and how grateful we are and also about what we need and want to do to keep it alive."

Dianna pauses and takes a breath and then continues.

"I could talk about this all day. It is my second favorite thing to do. My first is to be in that loving state with Michael. Nothing in this life is as wonderful as that. Yes, life can be pretty great sometimes but this feeling, this experience never disappoints me and it is always incredible. But let me get back to the topic of intimacy, the radical type. We both like that word, radical, because it seems to come close to what we experience together. To me it feels mysterious in the sense that it takes me out of my ordinary way of feeling and being in life. I look at him and he looks at me, and some protective part of me drops away, and I can see that the same thing is happening to him, and I feel totally exposed with him and safe at the same time. I can feel it right now as I am talking about it. (She takes a deep breath and continues) I know the word vulnerable is sort of accurate for this but it is not strong enough to really describe what happens. Yes, we are both vulnerable in these moments but it is a magnificent vulnerability. It has majesty in it. It is both precious and powerful at the same time and it carries us closer than either of us ever thought two people could ever be and then it builds and builds and we kind of explode in a burst of love and joy, and I guess that is when ecstasy occurs. Now I need to take a moment. I am shaking from this."

Michael puts his arm around her, pulls her close and kisses her cheek.

"God I love this woman! You are so beautiful when you share this way!"

Chapter 12

Anger, Romantic Love and Radical Intimacy

It is a common belief among psychotherapists of all sorts, that anger is a normal ingredient in all healthy couples' relationships, including romantic love. Couple's therapists think this way especially and spend great effort teaching partners how to fight fairly. However, the real truth about anger in a couple's relationship is that it is almost never truly healthy and is almost always a result of immaturity and/or dysfunction.

It is a fact, of course, that most couples get angry and fight but this does not necessarily imply that anger is either healthy or desirable. It may be true that the popular attitude about the necessity of anger in relationship is actually a contributing factor to the high rate (approximately 50%) of divorce. Anger hurts and anger damages and anger distances. None of these rather predictable affects is helpful to the creation of a close and respectful connection between two lovers. Anger is almost always anathema to intimacy because it usually produces fear and either attack, withdrawal or a form of freezing. Intimacy, especially the radical sort that belongs with romantic love, requires significant and sustainable safety. Safety must infuse the very context of a couple's relationship in order for emotional intimacy to grow and blossom. Anger and safety are almost always experienced as opposites.

Romantic love has the power to create an experience of safety that is stronger and more intense than anything either lover has ever encountered. If that safety is then grown, deepened and nurtured by the various practices and attitudes of radical intimacy, a couple can enter and sustain a loving relationship that is transforming at every level. In order to do this each partner must surrender all weapons of destruction and anger should, must, be the first to go.

Anger is destructive, especially in a couple's relationship, because it usually arises out of immaturity and/or dysfunction. The childish, immature part of us is the part that reacts with anger when misunderstood or mistreated. It is the child that needs to be right or needs to have his or her way. It is the child that throws various forms of tantrums in an attempt to control and manipulate others. It is the dysfunctional or wounded part of us that misinterprets and overreacts to perceived harm and hurt. It is the wounded one that attacks and asks questions later. And on occasion, it is the individual who is both immature and wounded who uses anger as regular currency in communication because it is the emotion they feel most at ease with.

When a weapon of destruction such as anger appears in a love relationship both partners normally search for protection, and defenses are quickly constructed. If anger persists, walls get stronger and taller and eventually vulnerability is a tragic casualty of interpersonal war. Once vulnerability disappears, romantic love loses its hold and the couple begins the sad slide into co-existence. Co-existence, a state of living alongside but not deeply connected to one's partner, is the breeding ground for boredom, dissatisfaction, disappointment and greater and greater distance. As distance increases and each partner mourns the loss of the wonder that used to be, anger burns hotter and hurt intensifies and love gives way to resentment and even hate.

Anger then, is no friend to romantic love. If the ecstasy of romantic love is to live and prosper, each partner must learn to relate as a mature and healthy adult who can respond to difficulties without weapons or attack. Otherwise, even the most sacred and heart filled love will dissipate and die in the darkness that unmanaged anger creates.

Chapter 13

Dianna and Michael – Anger and Romantic Love

Michael stands up abruptly and begins to move around the room. He seems very intense about this subject.

"I really want to speak about anger. Is that OK with you, Sweetheart? (He looks intently at Dianna and she nods her agreement, clearly aware that Michael is passionate about the subject.)

"Thanks, Honey. I am so filled with energy about the issue of anger; I might actually feel angry about it. (He pauses and laughs at himself and continues.) I used to think, no, I used to believe, that anger was not only a normal part of a loving relationship but it was also necessary. I was convinced that learning to feel and express anger could make a real contribution to a healthy connection between two lovers. I bought everything that group leaders and therapists taught about it and I did everything I could to get in touch with my anger and to communicate it directly to my partner, and everyone else for that matter. In addition to that, I also encouraged my partner to get her anger out and not hold on to it. We both thought and believed that this was the way to relationship health and strength. I was wrong. I was dead wrong and I paid a terrible price for it. So did she. Anger destroyed us. Her anger and my anger killed whatever chance we had to make it work. We expressed it differently but we felt it and lived it and never learned to face and change what it was really doing to our rather fragile connection, and it burnt us up.

"Now, I want to make one thing clear. Anger is a reality, everyone feels it, and it should not be denied or avoided. If it is denied and avoided it will sink out of sight and still do its damage. But, and this is a very large BUT, anger in a relationship is extremely dangerous and must be attended to with care and maturity and love. It cannot be allowed to grow. It must be identified and worked on as if it is a form of relationship cancer. It cannot be given a permanent place in a romantic relationship. It must be treated like a destructive element that needs our immediate attention."

Michael pauses and takes a deep breath and continues.

"When I reflect on what I was taught for decades by professionals about anger, I think they were doing their best to deal with a powerful energy that was so prevalent that they simply decided that it was normal. But that sort of thinking would be like deciding that racism was normal because it was so prevalent in the South. Just because something shows up a lot does not mean it belongs nor has a right to exist. That is a child's logic and anger requires an adult response.

"Anger creates hurt and harm and distance. We cannot get close to an angry person. That is an observable fact. If I want you to come closer to me then I have to drop my anger in order to make it safe for both of us. If I don't do that then you move away and our intimacy suffers from it. If anger is present in a loving relationship then it is crucial for both partners to deal with it with understanding and compassion and get help if necessary. It must be seen as an unwanted guest and not a permanent boarder."

Dianna takes his hand and gently pulls him down beside her.

"Sweetheart, you are so passionate about this subject and I know it is because you have been so hurt by it. I have not had the same experience of anger as you have but it was definitely present in my relationship and it caused big problems also. The anger you encountered was hot, explosive and frequent. My experience was with repressed anger that showed up as sarcasm, brief but hurtful judgments, and coldness. It was almost never explosive but it was really hurtful and it created a very large emotional gap between us that grew and grew until there was only empty space. We had no intimacy at all, and then it was over.

"But then you and I met and fell in love and we shared so much about all sort of things and we both agreed that we wanted to create a relationship that contained as little anger as possible. We both see our love as far too precious to allow anger or any other negative emotion to damage it. And the amazing thing, Sweetheart, is that we have been able to do that. I feel so safe with you and I never worry about you attacking me or yelling at me or cursing me. You have not done that once in all the time we have been together. Not once, and I love you for that."

Michael responds.

"Yes, Sweetheart, you are right and you get lots of credit for that also. I know you get frustrated with me sometimes but you are always gentle with your communication and I love you for that too. In fact, you treat me so dearly that it makes me want to do the same for you. I can have a pretty nasty mouth on some occasions and cursing is certainly part of my repertoire, but I would actually be horrified if I spoke to you with disrespect. I never felt that way about another human being, not ever. The truth is, I love how we are together. We bring out the very best in each other and I give thanks for that all the time. I feel that my love for you is far more important than any other emotion I could have. That realization makes all the difference when I am upset about something. I am able to protect our love from any negativity that runs around in my head and I feel wonderful about that."

Dianna indicates that she wants the last word on this issue and Michael agrees.

"Michael, you said it so accurately. Anger is not welcome between us. We do get angry about other things and at other people but our connection is sacred and we protect it with both our hearts and minds. We can count on each other for that and it makes our bond truly strong. I love how we love each other, Sweetheart, and I know you do too."

Chapter 14

Intimacy, Especially Radical Intimacy, is for Adults

Radical intimacy is a form of sharing and exposing oneself that requires courage and depth. To truly open our heart to another individual, even if we are wonderfully in love with that person, is initially rather scary. Who we are is all we have, and what if our lover rejects us? This is a frightening possibility that we all encounter at each stage of radical intimacy. Each time we approach a new level of self-revelation and begin to offer our tender and vulnerable self to the one who is the most important person in our world, we quake a bit inside and hope with everything we are that we will be welcomed with compassion and understanding. We hope that our hidden self, now exposed, will not be judged as inadequate or crazy or alien or unacceptable but embraced and even loved. When this miraculous moment occurs, when this grace filled event happens, we find a joy unknown to lesser relationships. We see ourselves, no longer through our own clouded and often judgmental eyes, but now through the shining vision of one who loves all that we are even in our brokenness and imperfection. This event, at that sacred moment, can be the most healing and transforming moment of our entire lives. In truth, this is a miracle only possible within the safe and loving boundaries of radical intimacy and that kind of intimacy can only be found between two adults.

It takes two adults to enter and successfully manage the powerful energies of deep intimacy. Romantic love brings every couple to its door, granted, but only mature adults can navigate its complexities. Children in adult bodies lack the self-control, wisdom, courage and depth to meet its challenges and take full advantage of its opportunities. Too many couples, awash in the wonder of their new found ecstasy, run blindly into this new territory and quickly become confused and frightened at what they encounter. Then, they just as quickly convince themselves that this place is not for them and quickly retreat to safer levels of connection. They never seem to realize that the difficulty is not in the special level of intimacy they have just discovered but in their own inability to meet its requirements. If they could stop and take a more honest look at themselves, they might find a way to grow up and into the new possibilities, and there find an entirely new sense of each other and the love that they share.

Many couples fall deeply in love and then crash to the point of disillusionment when they encounter the possibilities of radical intimacy as offered them by their romantic encounter. They blame it on many things, too numerous to name here, but blame they do, instead of admitting that they either simply do not know how to relate effectively or are just too afraid to bare their deeper selves to each other. In either case, paradise is lost and the relationship slides into mediocrity or toxicity and divorce.

The elephant in the room of romance is too often immaturity. Only grownups can ride the ship of romantic love all the way to the shores of paradise. Children in adult bodies become awkward and giggly in the face of intense intimacy and make jokes about something they should honor. Worse, some create a story that it is unnecessary and only for the needy or too feminine. The gigglers retain the potential of growing into adults who can manage the tender intensities that love offers them, but the ones who condemn vulnerability are often doomed to a lifetime of shallow and unsatisfying relationships.

Romantic love is akin to lightning. It strikes where it will without any apparent consideration for age or maturity. It can take over the heart of a 19 year old as well as someone who is 90 with the same urgency and passion. We may make our hearts open to it but we cannot control when and if it strikes. It does not bargain and it does not offer any warning. When it arrives, it brings great desires and expectations and it is up to us to live up to its potentialities. The more mature and adult we are or are ready to become, the better we will do in its grasp. Then, it will carry us to heights of love and healing and ecstasy we have never imagined.

Chapter 15

Dianna and Michael – Radical Intimacy

Dianna gestures to Michael and suggests he begin.

"OK, Sweetheart. I will start on this one. I have quite a few thoughts on this subject but they seem to be mostly negative. Not about us, but about so many couples I have known who fell in love and then messed it up so badly they eventually destroyed what could have been a beautiful thing. It is super to watch two people find that special person and go goo-goo eyed with each other. Then it is really sad to watch them begin to act immature and say and do insensitive and hurtful things to each other. I hate that.

I remember once telling my friend that if he kept talking to his girlfriend that way he was going to screw the whole thing up. He just laughed and said she was not that sensitive and it would be fine. Well she started talking to him the same way and he got angry and called her names and it went to crap so fast they were both shocked. If they had not gone for couples counseling (at my insistence) they would have broken up. They are better now but they still lapse into childish behavior on occasion and I know it will come back to haunt them. And it seems that the shine is gone from their connection. I doubt they will ever get it back. It is too bad because they really had something."

Dianna picks up the conversation when Michael pauses.

"Honey, I know. You know too. We have both been there. We were guilty of that in past relationships and we paid a price for it. You know that. I am so happy we learned from it and now we both try hard to stay adult when it counts. I see the same thing happen with some of my friends too. Someone gets irritable about something and the other reacts in a childish way and neither one seems able to stop. Both of them end up getting hurt and a gap begins to form between them. They don't seem to know how to fix it so they just stop talking about it and hope things will get better if they avoid it. They convince themselves that this works but it doesn't. The hurt and anger just go underground and the distance increases. They are not as close as they used to be and it shows in so many ways including their sex lives. Then my friend comes to me to talk about how unhappy she is and I make suggestions but that seldom helps. It seems like too much work to make it better and they just keep on that way. I feel sad about that also."

Michael agrees with Dianna and continues to share.

"Honey, I see that too. Yes, I feel sad about it also. I have thought for years that it is too bad that the school system does not have courses on relationship. It would be great if there were classes on dealing with love and learning to listen and understand each other and how to deal productively with anger and misunderstanding. It would be incredible if there was a class about how important and powerful it can be if a person learns to live and relate as a mature adult. I mean something like making a list of the characteristics of being an adult and then discussing this in a high school or middle school class. Fantastic! But that does not occur and so we all have to learn this stuff from our own mistakes and that causes a lot of pain to lots of people. And, yes, Honey. I am really glad too that you and I learned from our own mistakes and do our best to be caring, mature adults in our relationship. It makes things so easy between us."

Note to Reader: To receive my Couples Radical Intimacy Exercises free, please email me at DrA@Mattcoyote.com Put "Radical Intimacy" in the subject line.

Chapter 16

Radical Intimacy as a Path to Healing, Growth and Ecstasy

Radical intimacy, an undefended and mutual self-revelation between two adult individuals who have come to see one another through the eyes of love, is a one-of-a-kind path into healing, inner growth and ecstasy that is not available in any other relationship. The experience of falling in love is universal and appears to be as old as human existence. And falling in love always contains an opportunity for deep and satisfying intimacy or what I have called the eyes of love. But radical intimacy and its incredible blessings, does not always develop in the midst of romantic love. Radical intimacy seems to require the context of romantic love and its heart opening intensity and passion but not all couples are equipped to take full advantage of its potential treasures. However, when the circumstances are right, when two lovers are both willing and able, a gate opens and something truly mystical emerges.

Every individual desperately wants to be known and loved and affirmed in the deepest part of her or his being. We all search for this experience our entire lives. This need is at the essence of everything we do and all that we say, think and dream. Yet, it remains elusive and we encounter it piecemeal, here and there, in ways that offer us a glimpse of that divine gift but never full on, and so we search and struggle on hoping that something or someone will someday appear and take our trembling hand and lead us to that pool of sacred water that will finally soothe our aching hearts.

The good news is that there is a path to this heart healing experience and that path is radical intimacy within the context of romantic love. It may be that radical intimacy can exist between two individuals who are not in love but there is no ready evidence of it. It seems that romantic love alone provides the passion and intensity, plus the new vision of the beloved required to open the gate to an intimacy that is beyond the bounds of anything available in any other form of relationship.

What then occurs when two romantically driven individuals truly surrender to the power of this kind of process? Much of what occurs is not linear and much happens simultaneously and quite a bit of it is mystical and thus ineffable, but all of it deserves at least an attempt at description.

The initial experience of romantic love might be compared to being swept up by a tidal wave, a force of nature so gigantic and overwhelming that there is no thought of resistance, only a feeling of being transported up and away from what you knew into something that is completely beyond what you expected. Then bang, you are set down on a beach naked, right in front of someone who has arrived the same way and is in exactly the same state. Your eyes meet and the idea of past lives, completely foreign to you before this moment, now seems entirely viable because you know, and your new lover knows, that you have known each other, deeply and intimately, a thousand times before.

Here it begins, on that light filled beach, a moment in which all defenses are dropped and fear of exposure is nowhere to be found and love dominates and permeates every cell of your bodies and you realize that this person is the one, the one who can see you. This is the one who can see the you that you have always hoped would be and could be seen and accepted and celebrated and loved, and you look now through new eyes and you see the glorious beauty of your lover in the same way she or he sees you, and all of creation sings and claps its hands at your reunion.

Yes, it begins in ecstasy and that ecstasy wants to remain. It does not want to become a shooting star that passes briefly through the dark sky of your life and then disappears into a sweet but irreclaimable past. That ecstasy wants to be the frequent companion of you who have become the blessed victims of that grace filled wave. It wants you to open your hearts to each other so deeply and with such care and tenderness that you will both become the beauty this love has let you see.

Chapter 17

Dianna and Michael – More on Radical Intimacy

Dianna speaks first.

"I suppose I should go first since you started the last comments on radical intimacy. The phrase seems somewhat intellectual to me but it is really important and deserves more attention. I love the image of a light filled beach where two people meet and open themselves to each other without fear. Being in love truly makes it possible to risk being radically open. Oops! I used the word, but it is accurate. Radical means going to the source and that is what happens when you and I connect, Honey. I did not know I had such a wonderful source of love until we met and our sharing, our special ecstasy, has taught me to have an entirely new level of respect for what lives in the deepest parts of my heart. This may sound strange but it is impossible to hold on to self-hate when I know that something that precious and sacred exists in me."

When Michael hears Dianna's last comment, he speaks up with enthusiasm.

"Honey, that is so profound! You are so right! Romantic love gives us the ability to become radically intimate with our lover and that level of intimacy puts us into contact with a sacred source of love. When we experience this we must reconsider who we are and what we are capable of in the highest and best sense. You are so right about that. How can I hate or denigrate who I am if such a beautiful energy lives in my heart? You nailed it, Sweetheart!"

Chapter 18

Radical Intimacy and Power

Radical intimacy is only possible with a peer. Any disparity in power, real or perceived, will cause a holding back that is the result of fear. Imagine, for example, that you are an employee and your boss wants to befriend you. If you enter into this relationship you will be unable to relax and be fully yourself or speak your whole truth because it might affect your job. Conversely, as the boss you must be careful not to impart any sensitive business information because it might shape that employee's feelings or perception of you or jeopardize other business relationships. The limitations of this situation may be evident to most of us as it pertains to a work environment but it also applies to a love relationship in which one person has more power than the other.

If one partner feels he or she is inferior or superior to the other then sharing cannot be horizontal and thus will not be free and uncensored. The inferior partner will hold back from fear and the superior partner will hold back because the other (inferior) person may not be perceived as capable of holding, tolerating or understanding his or her most private information. These perceptions of an inferior or superior partner affect many intimate relationships, even when romantic love is present, and always significantly limit the depth and breadth of sharing.

All true intimacy is horizontal. One who assumes the position of supe-riority will not share "down" because the lower partner will not be seen as deserving or "up to" the communication. One who assumes the posi-tion of inferiority will not share "up" because he or she may perceive her sharing as worthy of the superior person or that this person may use it against her. When sharing is not horizontal or mutual the issue of power permeates the relationship. When power is not equal and balanced then fear begins to cause filtering and facades arise and vulnerability recedes.

Radical intimacy opens the heart ever more deeply and makes space for love to enter and expand. A partially open heart is only partially able to give or receive love. A closed heart is unable to give or receive love and will often substitute attachment and confuse it with love. Attachment is a form of dependency and both ways of relating block the possibility of real intimacy or the true sharing of love.

Fear is the enemy of intimacy. It is especially harmful and limiting to radical intimacy which requires a fully open and undefended heart and the deepest levels of self-revelation combined with a response to one's partner that is unconditionally accepting, compassionate and re-ciprocal. Once fear takes hold, each partner begins to censor and share partial information. Secrets invade the sacred space of relationship and intimacy begins to shrink.

The great and most effective equalizer between any two individuals, and especially in a romantic relationship, is vulnerability. It is the opening of the heart and the exposing of the tenderest, most secret, wounded, most protected, frightened and/or precious and treasured aspects of one's inner being. It is then the welcoming, compassionate, understanding and non-judgmental receiving gesture of the other that completes the circle and the experience of radical intimacy. Then it must be continued at the same or deeper level of vulnerability by ones partner. This creates a dynamic flow of intimacy that can then take both partners into what might be called radical intimacy.

Chapter 19

Dianna and Michael – Radical Intimacy and Power

Dianna pats Michael on the shoulder and tells him to go for it. He smiles and starts talking.

"Honey, you know I love this subject. Thanks for letting me go first. I think a power balance is crucial between two lovers. It is important in any relationship but with lovers it is truly a big deal. If you have more power than me, I could be afraid of you and that would be tragic. I know couples who have this problem. For example, a man might be afraid of a woman due to the power of her anger. Anger can easily create a power imbalance if one person uses it a lot and the other is not good at it. Another common power imbalance might occur when one person makes all the money and the other does not work. This is a difficult issue for many couples and it often depends on how much they both respect and honor mothering. If the man works and the woman does not then both may assume her role is inferior to his. I know that many couples currently attempt to see this differently but the culture as a whole has not made the shift. It is still very difficult for women and their partners to value her mother-homemaker role as one equal to that of a man who has a traditional job."

Dianna indicates she is ready to comment.

"I have to confess that this was partially true for me. I stayed home and took care of the children for a few years and I did feel that I had less power than my husband because of it. We did not discuss it but I felt it and I am sure he did also. I am not entirely sure what we could have done about it. What do you think, Honey?"

Michael has a quick response to Dianna's question.

"I think vulnerability is the answer. You and I are consistently that way with each other and it keeps us close and balanced in our intimacy. When power is out of balance, being vulnerable makes all the difference. It levels the playing field, so to speak. When two people drop their defenses and open their hearts they lose the sense of superiority and inferiority. In fact, the issue of power disappears and love fills the space."

Dianna smiles and continues.

"That is well said, Sweetheart. Love fills the space, is right! Love has no room for anything but itself and shared vulnerability always invites love to pour in and fill both hearts. Wow, I am getting poetic here but it feels right to me. I think the solution to any power imbalance between two lovers is being very committed to being vulnerable every single day. That is a good idea for any love relationship but it really helps with the power problem also."

Michael agrees.

"You are exactly right, Honey. And, yes, you are poetic. Thanks for saying it so well!"

Chapter 20

Women, Equality and Intimacy.

For at least the last 5000 years, women have been seen as inferior to men by almost all cultures, political systems and religions. This perception has done enormous damage to and placed severe limitations on marriage and all other intimate relationships between men and women. As stated in other sections of this book, intimacy, especially the radical intimacy potentially present in romantic love, cannot grow and prosper if one partner is perceived as superior or inferior to the other. Intimacy requires an equality of power, otherwise, safety is diminished and closeness is limited or damaged.

When a man and a woman fall in love, the love itself is an invitation to a deep and transforming relationship between equals. Every romantic experience has offered this gift since the first two lovers fell into each other's arms. Sadly, only a small percentage have been able to take advantage of the immense blessing of radical intimacy that this particular form of love always promises. Too quickly and too easily, both partners fall prey to the pernicious perception that men are somehow superior. As soon as this nasty but ubiquitous idea takes hold then both lovers lose access to the deep waters of romantic love and are relegated forever to the baby pool of intimacy. Both partners may be unaware of the subtle shift but both eventually suffer from the shallowness of connection. Instead of continuing on a mystical journey of loving discovery and the realization of the great potentials of romantic love, they settle for mediocrity and even boredom. Then, with no true depth of bonding, the once loving couple becomes highly vulnerable to the difficulties of life and the dissolution of their relationship becomes a real and present possibility.

It would be easy to blame men for the persistent perception of inequality between the sexes. That conclusion would, however, be both sophomoric and ultimately a waste of time. The truth is there have been a thousand reasons for this unfortunate concept and men and women alike have subscribed to it for millennia. Solutions to social problems, especially those that involve intimate relationships, are never found in blame. Blame creates victims and victims perceive themselves as powerless. The real solution begins with honesty and vulnerability. Both men and women need to admit to this sad state of perception and then open their hearts to each other in a radical new way. Love, once fully invited, will do the rest.

Chapter 21

Michael and Dianna – Women, Equality and Intimacy

Dianna begins with a brief but important question for Michael.

"Honey, have you ever thought of me as inferior to you because I am a woman?"

Michael laughs a strong, good-natured laugh.

"Sweetheart, the truth is that has never been an issue for me. I have always seen women and men as equals. I think that has something to do with my grandmother and mother. Their relationships with my grandfather and father had no signs of being less or more. Strange given their generations but that was the way it was from my early years. I also never saw women and men as basically different. To me, they are exactly the same right beneath the surface. Tell me, Honey, have you ever felt that I treated you as inferior to me or acted superior to you in any way?"

Dianna smiles and shakes her head.

"NO, Honey, not at all. It is one of the things I love about you. You never treat me as less than you and you never make any sexist comments or jokes, and I really appreciate that. I always find that obnoxious when men do that and even worse when women do it. You don't even make blonde jokes. How unusual is that? You and I have had many conversations about this subject and you frequently say that part about women and men being the same. I know you mean it but so many people think that is not true. You know, they write books and do videos about it and so many people think they are correct."

Michael nods in agreement and begins to speak forcefully.

"Honey, you are so right about that. Lots of professionals make lots of money talking about the differences between the sexes. They do big business emphasizing the trivial differences. But the truly powerful stuff is in the similarities. Our hearts are the same. Our deepest needs are the same. Our hurts and joys and loves and fears are the same. Once a man understands this about a woman he has a key to her heart and the same goes in the other direction.

"Another way of explaining this is to change the wording a little and the truth becomes clear. I like to think of it this way. The unconscious man and the unconscious woman are different, from different planets, as they say. But once a man and a woman wake up and begin to really know themselves, they are far less controlled or defined by cultural images and beliefs. Then they can relate from their hearts and souls without gender role confusion and imbalance. This is not easy to do but it can be done and you and I are a great example of that.

"When I hold you close and look into your eyes, I see someone special and sacred and precious and it would be incredibly stupid of me to consider you inferior. In fact, sometimes I have to watch myself or I will think of you as superior. (He laughs and continues) Your heart is so loving, sometimes I have to work to keep up. But that is not about being male or female. It is about seeing you as a blessing. I think you know that."

Dianna smiles and responds.

"I love the way you look at me, especially when we are making love. I see you the same way Honey. I often cry in the midst of it all when our eyes meet that way. I know this could sound sappy to some people but I really don't care. It is not sappy to us. It is incredibly beautiful and I would not give it up for anything. I would be devastated if either of us began to mess this up by deciding that one of us was superior or inferior!"

Michael nods enthusiastically in agreement.

"Sweetheart, I am completely with you on this one. I feel so bad for men who persist in holding on to ignorant anachronisms. OK, too much head stuff there! I feel sorry for guys who think women are inferior. As soon as a guy thinks that, he can no longer be deeply intimate with a woman he loves. The same goes for the women who buy into that paradigm also.

"Once again, I think the antidote to this imbalance is being radically open and vulnerable with the one you love. That means to open your heart and allow your lover to see your naked, wonderful and messy self in all its glory. The truth is this is where the eyes of love make a difference because when we are in love we see the real beauty of our partner. No imbalance there. Only wonder!"

Chapter 22

Love and Lust

Every full on experience of romantic love involves lust but every experience of lust does not involve love. This is a rather obvious truth that is evident to most adults. It is only the immature mind that confuses the two and imagines that every lustful encounter could be love. It is important to note, however, that love without lust cannot qualify as romantic. This sort of love would be defined as platonic and is not to be confused with the whole body, heart, mind and soul experience of romantic love. Lust must be present for the entire romantic connection to occur but cannot be the single driving force of a relationship. It is a fire starter but not a fire sustainer. Without the accompanying full engagement of heart and mind and soul, lust fizzles with the orgasm, and an empty space emerges between sex partners.

Lust is a sign of positive physical chemistry between two potential lovers and is an excellent starting point. Without it, romance will very probably not appear even if both partners hope for it. If lust is not present, it is usually advisable for a couple to consider friendship as a possible option rather than romance. If, however, lust is present and intense then it is important to use its energy to explore the attraction in much greater depth. Couples, who take the time and make the effort to go deeper, have the best possibility of an authentic romantic connection. If their romance has space to blossom then their lust will usually follow suite and intensify exponentially.

In this newly developing age of radical intimacy between two equal partners, love and lust can greatly enhance each other in new and exciting ways. Lust brings wonderful intensity to a physical encounter. If this intensity is matched by and held in a context of passionate sharing of souls and hearts, both lovers will be transported to a level of ecstasy that is unavailable to any other human relationship. Lust will become more than a physical experience and will expand into a passionate desire to encounter and know one's lover at greater and greater depths. Each partner will begin to experience an additional kind of lust for emotional and spiritual connection that equals and may even exceed the drive to enjoy and explore the other's body. As these new and deeper encounters occur, their energy gives back to and enhances sexual intimacy, and builds a circle of ever intensifying passion that cannot be achieved by lust or love alone.

Chapter 23

Dianna and Michael − Love and Lust

Michael indicates that he would like to speak first on this issue.

"I think the relationship between love and lust is really crucial for any couple who fall in love. It is the match that lights the forest fire. I will never forget the moment I fell in lust with you, Sweetheart. We were sitting at a restaurant and meeting face to face for the first time. We talked for a while and then for some reason we both leaned closer to each other and I looked directly into your eyes. I knew that I found you attractive before that moment. But, that moment was explosive for me. When our eyes made contact I could not breathe. What I felt for you was so incredibly intense that it seemed to explode all the way from my eyes to every other part of my body. It was heat and fire and it shook me to my core and I actually felt briefly that I would pass out. Wow. I can feel a bit of it now. I knew in that moment that I had to see you and be close to you again soon and that this was different than anything I ever felt for any woman, ever. Yes, it was clearly sexual. I wanted you. Boy, did I want you. It is probably good that we were in a public place because I might have given you a passionate kiss and embrace right then and I am not sure you were ready for that at that moment. Wow, I still feel it. Maybe you could talk now, Honey."

Dianna laughs and kisses Michael on the cheek and takes up the conversation.

"Honey, I know I say it over and over but I love your passion. It makes me want to eat you up. But that will have to wait. I want to respond to your sharing. I felt very physically attracted to you that day but our first kiss was the moment I sort of exploded with lust for you. After that it seems we have been pretty equal in our passion and lust for each other. I also want to say that I completely agree with you about becoming lustful for each other emotionally and spiritually. For me they have actually merged into one package. I really love it when we make deep and loving emotional connection. When we share our hearts I almost always feel a twinge of sexual energy for you. And when we combine emotional connection with sex something spiritual often occurs and I feel so close to you and to God at the same time. You and I get the same way when that occurs. We both begin to cry or even sob with joy and relief and I guess this is what true ecstasy is. It is incredible and so wonderful that I have come to believe that this is the best and highest purpose of romantic love."

Michael asks for the final word on this issue and Dianna smiles her consent.

"You said that really well, Honey. Combining lust with deep vulnerable emotional sharing and heart filled love can produce really profound spiritual experiences. It is fantastic and you are fantastic and we are fantastic. I am so grateful we fell in love and that we nurture it so beautifully. "

Chapter 24

The Bed of Love

Two people decide to have a sexual encounter.

They enter a bed together and it happens.

What occurs is based on the bed they have chosen.

Some choose a bed of lust; hot, urgent, mindless and often without heart.

Others find themselves in a bed of friendship; convenient, safe and without commitment.

Many choose a bed some call the cheater's bed,

Some, that of an affair, desperate for connection, attention, novelty,

Release from the grey sameness of an insipid marriage.

Then there are those who seek the bed of a stranger,

Met quickly in a bar or a party, mind and heart unknown

But ready to use and be used for a night.

There are many kinds of beds that define sexual interaction between two individuals

But there is only one Bed of Love.

The Bed of Love is for lovers who are willing to be naked first with their hearts and souls.

They know that physical nakedness alone is a cheap substitute

For the ecstasy that occurs in a bed saturated with the volcanic juices of heart and soul.

They are unwilling to cheat themselves of the life changing wonders

That accompany the deep joining of lovers who open their hearts before they open their bodies.

They understand the real essence of nakedness and have not confused it with nudity.

They drop pretense and shed their defenses.

They abandon shallowness and games and bare their true selves.

They risk the most precious parts of themselves, and once lovingly received,

They are ready for the tender touching, opening and entering of hand and legs

And hard and wet parts,

Each one affirming the beauty that they are part of together.

Anything less than this is not acceptable in the true Bed of Love.

Chapter 25

The Eyes of Love

Romantic love is the every-person's opportunity to experience divine grace and as such it brings a gift that has numinous (divine) qualities. Grace falls like rain and soaks the heart of one who is then blessed with this love. This grace, this love, brings us a gift of new sight by which we can see the Other, our Beloved, with divine eyes. In this state of heightened awareness, we are able to see our Beloved as she truly is, in all her wonder and beauty, and she, lifted and filled with the same love, can see us as we are. In these sacred moments we no longer see with our natural eyes but with our Heart which is the center of True Sight. It is from this vantage point that all the glory of our lover is revealed to us.

It is the heart's great desire to be seen this way. It is here that all our doubts about being lovable and valuable drop away. Through the grace-filled eyes of our lover we come to know our best and highest self and are carried up in an intense yearning to rise to, become, reveal and celebrate that awareness. At the very same instant that this self-revelation occurs, we also see our Beloved for who she is in her highest and best self. We want to do everything we can to nurture her and give to her so that she can sustain her precious being.

Romantic love, and its gift of the eyes of love, is not earned and, like rain, it falls on every heart. We cannot choose or cause it but once soaked by its divine dew we can only surrender to its transformative power. If we try to resist we will find ourselves torn into pieces. If we accept our fate we will be given an experience of wholeness that is worth whatever price love may ask of us. That precious wholeness can only be seen through the eyes of love and it is up to us to nurture and sustain that sight as we love and live with our Beloved.

Every person who has ever fallen in love has had an experience of the eyes of love. But for most, that glorious vision of the Beloved quickly dims and then is only a memory. It is then, too often relegated to an experience of intoxication, and is interpreted as an imagined and unrealistic perception of another person created by the distortive energies of emotion and lust. Many of these same couples yearn to revisit this experience but both believe that it cannot be revived and lack the skills to reconnect with it. The good news is that the eyes of love need not dim and both partners can learn to sustain and nurture this wonderful vision of the Beloved.

Chapter 26

THE EYES OF LOVE: A Correction

I want to begin with a quote about love from an author I deeply respect and then I want to tell you why he is absolutely wrong. In fact, he is so wrong I feel like yelling in his face and telling him he has no frigging idea about what love really is? Am I angry? You bet I am because this highly educated Jungian analyst has written some very insightful stuff and lots of people read his work. That means quite a few individuals and couples will read these lines and swallow them whole and tragically miss out on the wonderful treasure they are experiencing.

So what is the terrible quote? Here it is.

"The "in-love" state, great narcotic as it is, numbs consciousness, retards growth and serves as a soporific to the soul."

By the way, "soporific" means something like a sedative. Which in this case is redundant given his previous use of the word narcotic.

Why does this quote by the writer/analyst James Hollis irritate me so intensely? In truth is he not simply stating what many people already believe about the "phase" called romantic bliss? Yes, this is a version of the traditional belief about the first stage of being in-love. But this interpretation is not only wrong but also terribly misleading because to speak this way with such simplistic and condemning conviction will lead many lovers to lose one of the greatest gifts love has to offer: THE EYES OF LOVE.

The experience of falling in love is not a narcotic. To call it that is to commit a sacrilege. It is in fact the exact opposite of a mind numbing drug. Falling in love opens our eyes more clearly than any other experience of life. Falling in love gives us the ability to see another person's astounding magnificence. Our love-eyes allow us to see what has always been present but was hidden. We, with love-eyes, look upon our lover and see her or his true beauty and true wondrousness.

Falling in love tears away the blindfold of normal vision and graces us with the ability to see the loved other as the masterpiece of art that they actually are and always have been. One blessed look and we are changed forever. Who and what we see suddenly becomes almost a god and being with that person assumes a quality much like worship.

Is this a narcotic? Only to the cynic who does not look carefully enough to see what is really occurring. Yes, many would say, *"But this wonderful phase never lasts. It always dissipates in the harsh light of reality and we go back to the regular difficulties of relationship.*" I will acknowledge that most couples lose touch with this very special experience in less than 12 months, BUT, not because it is a drug that wears off. It wears off because the once blessed and happy couple has no idea about how to sustain it and even expect it to go away. This when the eyes of love begin to go blind (not the other way around as the love-is-blind cynics love to call it) and neither partner knows what to do to recover their precious love sight.

Falling in love brings new sight and that sight opens us to the ultimate truth about another person. Each of us is an astounding work of art, a masterpiece beyond compare. Yet we live our lives sadly unaware of our magnificence until for a brief and blessed time some previously ordinary individual is given the eyes to see who we truly are. And then we are given the same eyes through which to return the favor.

How does this miracle occur? I think of it as grace and I also think that grace is poured out on all humanity from time to time and even the lowliest among us can feel its cleansing balm that opens our eyes to something only God usually sees.

The first good news is that falling in love comes to many if not most of us. The second good news is that it does not have to end. If we are willing to put aside our cynicism and our long held belief that love always crashes down into the hard realities of life, we can learn how this wonder can be sustained and we can then be blessed with years of romantic bliss.

Chapter 27

Dianna and Michael – The Eyes of Love

Both Michael and Dianna indicate great enthusiasm on this subject and after a moment of brief communication, Dianna speaks first.

"I love this idea of the eyes of love. I really love it because it truly describes my experience. Falling in love with you also means seeing your highest and best self and that self, my darling, is so precious I could kiss you all over when I look at you that way! (Dianna laughs and pauses and then continues) OK, I know I get mushy about this but it would really be strange if I acted cool and heady about it. This is the good stuff. It is what lovers ache for and here it is, real and true and squeezable! I see you, Baby. I really see who you are and you are better than fantastic.

Love gives me the sight to see you and I never want to lose that vision."

Michael grins and blushes and begins to share.

"I am getting red now Sweetheart. You really got me this time! (He laughs and kisses her cheek) The wonderful part is that I see you the same way. I see your beauty that is far deeper than your lovely face. I see you are truly and incredibly special and glowing and it is why I have often teased you that you have little knobs on your back where the angel wings used to be. Wow, I am getting mushy too. I really never thought I could love someone this intensely but as we spend more and more time together my sight gets better and better and I can see more and more of your devastating beauty.

"OK, I used the word devastating because it is the most accurate word for what I experience when I see you in all your glory. Sometimes when I look at you something shatters in me. Something is ravaged and I think it is my old shabby vision of you. When I see you through the eyes of love, my ordinary eyes cannot hold what you are to me. My ordinary senses cannot tolerate your light. (He pauses) Yes, I know how this sounds but to say it with less grandeur would be disrespectful to how I see you. I cannot say it better. I see your true self and you, my dearest, are magnificent. I refuse to understate this, so here it is and here it will be." (He takes a big breath and kisses Dianna's lips)

Chapter 28

Why Does the Ecstasy of Romantic Love Disappear?

Merging: The Loss of the Other

All romantic intimacy requires an I and an Other. There must be a Me and a You (a not-me), otherwise I am relating to myself and the mystery and passion of connecting to someone else disappears. Two separate individuals meet, fall head over heels in love, and enter the ecstatic process of romantic love. They want to be close, make love, touch and feel, and listen and share, and that is what they do for the first weeks and months of their love affair. Then something changes and the intensity begins to diminish. and the excitement lessens and the loving becomes more mundane and finally they sit together at a restaurant in a bored silence and think about all they have to do when they get home or back to the office. What happened? What took them from ecstasy to boredom in a few months? Where and when did they lose the wonder that moved them both so deeply?

The answer to this very important question lies in the first sentence of the paragraph above. "All romantic intimacy (and thus all ecstasy and passion) requires an I and an Other." When the Other (not-me) begins to merge with the I (me), then the experience of intimacy lessens. Merging, here means a psychological process that almost always occurs when two people become very close, physically, mentally, and emotionally for an extended period of time. Boundaries blur and each person becomes less individual and more part of her or his partner. In a very real sense the not-me becomes so familiar that the experience of being different disappears and merging occurs. This process happens at different rates in different couples but few are immune to it.

When two individuals move in together, sleep together, make love, talk, work, play, eat, watch TV day after day, their relationship slowly assumes a predictability that may seem comfortable and safe but is actually the beginning of the merging process. Familiarity is the order of the day. One no longer surprises the other. Each thinks they know who the other is and how the other will respond or react to life and its challenges and opportunities. Attending to the responsibilities of daily life assumes priority over attending to the needs of the relationship and this imbalance contributes to merging.

As time passes and predictability and familiarity dominate, each partner loses a sense of the Other and intimacy on all levels disappears. Sex is no longer lovemaking and assumes a quality of mutual masturbation and tension release. Conversation is filled with who has to do what or who has done what to whom. When intimacy ceases boredom takes its place and what originally was a loving couple excited to be and live together dissolves into an automatic reaction machine without a real heart or spirit. At this point, merger is complete and in the worst sense the two have become one. It is at this point that something almost sinister occurs. Each partner begins to treat the other the same way they treat themselves.

Many couples, who began their relationship with romantic love, wonder why they say hurtful things to each other that they would never say to anyone else. Why do they curse and attack one another with such negative and often vicious behavior if this is the person they say they love the most? The answer can be found in the idea and the process of merger. When two individuals merge they lose the sense of an Other (not-me) and *begin to treat the Other as they treat themselves.* Here is how that works.

Most of us treat others better than we treat ourselves. We may never curse or yell at a stranger or even a friend but we often carry on a constant stream of negative self-talk that we rarely share with others. If we make a mistake or fail at something, even a small thing, we might berate ourselves and call ourselves names like 'stupid, idiot, dummy, moron, piece of crap', the list is endless. In the beginning of a romantic love affair we would never think of speaking to our dear and wonderful partner this way. That person is special and different and we protect them from our nasty and judgmental self-talk. But then we merge and lose the sense of being separate people, and then we begin to relate to our partner as if they are now inside us. At this point, their mistakes become ours and they are no longer protected from our internal nastiness. Suddenly we speak to them with the same hurtful and judgmental language we use on ourselves. Now merger has not only caused the loss of romance and intimacy, it has become a source of toxic behavior that can and often does, destroy any semblance of love.

When two individuals begin the process of merger, they each begin to discover how they really feel about themselves inside. If either person has a low level of self-esteem or a high level of self-hate, these feelings and thoughts will begin to dominate the relationship, and what was once beautiful will now become ugly and destructive. At this point many couples decide they have no option but the dissolution of their connection and divorce is the only path to peace.

Chapter 29

Dianna and Michael – Merging
and the Loss of the Other

Dianna indicates that she wants to speak first.

"Michael, you are the one who loves to talk about this subject so I think I will comment first and then let you do your thing, Honey. (She smiles warmly and Michael responds with the same affection). I used to worry a lot that we would lose the wonderful energy we had. It was so incredible to me and so special and I have always felt so grateful for our love. I never want to lose it and I know you don't either. We have talked so often about what merging is and how it kills the feeling of ecstasy, and I think I understand it intellectually. I mean, it makes sense to me that it takes two separate people to fall in love and be intimate and it also makes sense that those two can lose their boundaries when they live so closely together over time. I also get it that being close can lead to merging and then, in a way, the two become one and intimacy stops occurring."

Michael chimes in briefly.

"Sweetheart, that was really clear. You said the whole thing as good as I ever could."

Dianna laughs and continues.

"Thanks Honey. Yes, I do understand the concept but the real issue is how we make sure it does not happen to us. We have been together for quite a while now. A lot longer than a couple of years and, thank God, we are still crazy in love. I want us to talk about how we keep that level of loving alive, because we do and it is still as good or better than it was the first year."

Dianna pauses and looks pensive and then speaks again.

"I think we do quite a few things that help us see each other as separate people and those particular habits help sustain our passion for each other. One thing is that we actually talk about it. We want to nurture what is good between us so we avoid taking anything for granted. I wake up every morning grateful for you and I share that with you almost every day. You do the same with me. We have an ongoing conversation about our relationship and how much we love each other and how special and wonderful that is. I am sure that makes a difference. So many couples stop that sort of communication too soon and that makes them begin to take each other for granted and I think that contributes to merging. (She looks at Michael and he is agreeing enthusiastically).

"One of the best things we do is make an effort to be really intimate.

Yes, we have fantastic lovemaking, but I am talking about what you love to call radical intimacy. We are not afraid to look deeply into each other's eyes and allow our hearts to fill up with affection and appreciation for the other. We cry together that way often, I mean at least once a month or more. We don't hesitate to be what I call "mushy". We get vulnerable, undefended, touchy-feely, romantic, tender, all that stuff, a lot. You don't hesitate to be that way with me and much of the time you initiate it. Many men have a fear of that but you jump in, Honey, and I love you when you get that way. It never seems weak to me. In fact, it actually turns me on."

Dianna pauses and Michael begins to share.

"Honey, if you keep that up we will have to get a room! (They both laugh out loud). I want to respond to that last comment you made, not the turn on, but the statement about me as a man and being vulnerable. I think many men really have a fear of looking weak or too feminine and therefore avoid being vulnerable with their lover. It is a giant mistake and paradoxically they pay a worse price for not learning how. A man who holds back his deeper emotions of love and tenderness and gratefulness, and even need, is a man who deprives his lover (and himself) of closeness and loving connection and really incredible sex. And finally, his holding back cheats his lover of fully knowing who he is and that makes it even easier for her to become bored and boredom is a form of merging. We know what happens then, right? (Dianna nods in agreement).

"Let me take this merging idea a little further. Loving you is the best thing I have ever done in my life and I want that love to remain alive and vibrant and intense and beautiful for the rest of our existence together. Nothing is more important to me than loving you and guess what? Loving you makes every other aspect of my life better. My work is better and my play is better. I am more creative, more dedicated and more successful in every way. Loving you does not detract from who I am. Loving you makes me a better me. OK, I could go on about this but I think I am clear. I am convinced that what I have just said is at the core of what prevents our merging. It means I am attending to the quality of our relationship every single day and that commitment makes all the difference.

"So many couples fall in love and totally love the experience, and then amazingly forget to attend to it, and it dissipates like fog in sunlight. There is no frigging way I am going to allow that to happen. I have put our love under my protection and I will do whatever is necessary to keep it safe. (Michael pauses and takes a breath). I know I am intense about this but that is the truth. I want to protect our love and I know being merged, taking each other for granted, losing our romance, all of that, cannot be allowed to happen. So I have a hundred ways of loving and being with you that keep it wonderful.

"I am not going to name every one of those hundred ways right now, Honey, but I do want to share a few. I agree with everything you named when you began to share earlier . I just want to add a few more. One of the most important is I pay attention. I know this may sound simple but it is also powerful. Couples who stop paying attention lose touch with each other and merging occurs really fast when that happens. I know that people who stop paying attention to their lover begin to relate to them as a mental image, an idea of who they are, instead of the chang-ing, growing and surprising individual they actually are in the present. I know this could sound heady but it is true. We all form internal mental images of who we think people are and then we interact with the image instead of the real person. Once you become just an image to me then you disappear and I don't even realize it.

"So I pay attention every day. I watch how you walk and move and sit and laugh and dance and smell and talk and get frustrated or play with the dog…I could go on and on. I notice what you say and what you wear and I really pay attention to what you like and what you don't like in people and clothes and friends and food and weather and it goes on and on. And by paying attention to who you are and what you do and like and dislike and think I see you in the present and my image of you stays fresh and alive and that really helps me see you as a separate person who is special and precious to me. Wow, I do love to talk about this. I am going to take a break now, Sweetheart. Thanks for listening.

Chapter 30

Romantic Love and Merging

Falling in Love

The other is sacred and precious and is seen through the Eyes of Love.

Each partner sees the other as separate and unique.

Each partner has a compelling urge to bare their soul and heart to the other

and be affirmed and validated.

Each partner has an intense desire to give their best

and most valuable gift to the other – their love.

Being in the presence of the other is exciting, joyful and frequently ecstatic.

Sex is intimate, tremendously passionate, frequently ecstatic, always loving, and often spiritual.

Chapter 31

Romantic Love and Merging

Merging Begins

Attraction and affection draw partners to spend more and more time together.

Habituation enters the relationship.

The distinct sense of separateness and other begins to diminish.

Each partner begins to take the other for granted.

Co-dependency appears and grows.

Intimacy begins to be replaced by busyness and routine.

Chapter 32

Romantic Love and Merging

Merging Progresses

As psychological merging increases so do all the elements described in Slide 2 above.

Each partner continues to lose a sense of separateness.

Closeness loses its excitement

and takes on a quality of sameness and loss of intensity.

Partners lose most of the sense of a precious or sacred other and begin to treat each other with the same attitudes that dominate their attitudes about themselves internally.

Habituation increases to most areas of the relationship.

Chapter 33

Romantic Love and Merging

Merging Progresses to the Point of Severe Overlap

An almost complete state of psychological merger that results in loss of a true sense of an Other.

Sexual encounters are almost always an experience of mutual masturbation rather than making love.

Boredom from sameness dominates the relationship.

Partners often treat each other the way they treat themselves internally.

Any self-hate, low self-esteem or core dysfunction permeates and often dominates interaction between partners.

Radical intimacy and ecstatic experience cease to exist.

Chapter 34

Romantic Love and Merging

The Resurrection of Romantic Love

Couples begin the process of adding spontaneity, mystery, gratitude and savoring

 to their daily interaction.

Differentiation (a sense that there are once more two individuals present in the relationship) begins to grow.

Habituation is identified and attended to with love and creativity.

Both partners renew their commitment to holding the relationship and the other as sacred and precious.

Sexual encounters return to love making.

Radical intimacy is practiced regularly.

Affirmation and appreciation is voiced daily.

Ecstasy returns and romantic love is revived.

Chapter 35

Sustaining the Eyes of Love

Recently I wrote an article entitled THE EYES OF LOVE. In it I described the experience of falling in love (romantically) and my conviction that this gift of grace is available to any and all human beings. I also said that this gift can be squandered or destroyed if it is not received with care and consideration. Most lovers who are graced with this very wonderful experience, sadly lose their romantic connection (the eyes of love) within 3 to 18 months and seldom recover it for the duration of their relationship. This loss is so common that most couples expect it to occur and are not surprised when it dissipates. I consider this an unnecessary tragedy. The truth is that the state of ecstatic love between two lovers does not have to lessen, ever, and in fact can grow and blossom into something both magnificent and lasting. This state is what I believe is the intended end point of all romantic love and anything less becomes a settling, a compromise, a giving up before the full blessing is received and explored.

How then could this ultimately mystical experience be nurtured and sustained for a life time between two lovers? To be clear, sustaining the eyes of love is more art than science and is truly more a matter of heart than mind. However, some essential guidelines can be named and described. My list is not exhaustive and I imagine I will share more ideas on this subject in the future. For now be assured that each of these "ingredients" is crucial to the sustenance of the grace-filled gift I call the eyes of love. Each one is important and has its appropriate place in the life of a loving couple.

The gift must be seen as precious. Each partner must hold the relationship with the lover as the most precious thing in their life. Anything or anyone seen as precious will be treated with immense care and attention. It will assume a sacred quality that engenders an attitude approaching worship. This attitude will be held by both partners and will be a frequent topic of conversation both intimate and intellectual. It must be understood and experienced daily. When this occurs joy appears in ordinary interaction. Every touch is noticed and important. Every eye contact is meaningful and each simple act of living together becomes a blessing.

Gratefulness is the order of the day, every day. When one lover sees her or his partner through the eyes of love gratefulness is spontaneous. The heart fills and wants to speak and speaking becomes necessary for sustaining the blessing. Gratefulness cannot be taken for granted. It always comes as a part of the eyes of love but must be shared openly, frequently and with a vulnerable heart. Grace descends, fills us with love and that love must pass through the mouth as well as the eyes. It must be spoken to recreate itself. We must allow our hearts to speak our gratefulness to our partner with passion. When we open this way it seems that grace smiles on us and gives itself even more and our love for our partner expands our heart's capacity to receive and give beyond measure.

Sharing what we see. The eyes of love give us the special capacity to see who and what our lover truly is; blessed, gifted, unique, valuable, a treasure. If we see that truth and then share it with our lover, over and over and over again then we both bask in the light it generates. This sharing is healing, inspiring and renewing. It draws out the magnificence of our lover and in some ineffable way it fills the sharer with wonder. Nothing in this world heals and blesses our souls as powerfully as this sort of sharing.

Every word is a matter of tenderness. To lovers who see each other as precious every word that passes between them makes a difference. All communication passes through the filter of tenderness. Anything less than tenderness is unacceptable. All words have power and that power must be surrendered to love. Tenderness will transform all communication into messages that are clear and compassionate, helpful and rarely hurtful. Tenderness smoothes misunderstanding and gives rise to a generosity of spirit that resolves all perceived differences.

Chapter 36

Michael and Dianna – Eyes of Love

Michael begins in a very serious and pensive voice.

"I believe very deeply in this idea of the eyes of love. Yes, I used to think, just like everyone else, that it would come and go and I would have no control over it. I would enjoy it while it lasts and then accept its passing. I remember being overwhelmed by my feelings for you and the first time I looked, really looked into your eyes. The intensity was so great I stopped breathing for a moment. It was incredible. I did not expect it. I knew I found you attractive and interesting and all of that but for some reason I leaned closer to you across the table and bang!, lightening struck and my breath disappeared and I fell a rush of wild energy dance all over my body. God, I can feel it right now, Sweetheart. It was like being high but better, far better. And the truth is I still feel many versions of it when we are together in all sorts of situations. I thought I would only feel it when we were making love or dancing together or in some typical romantic situation but I was wrong and I am so glad I was wrong. I can really feel that way almost any time I decide to pay attention to you and allow my heart to open and that love dances. That is the best description I can find for the experience. My love dances wildly all through my body and I love you so much I could eat you up!"

Dianna responds as Michael pauses to take a breath.

"Honey, I know I sound like a broken record sometimes but I feel just like you do. Maybe that is one of the great things about this experience. We go so deeply into loving each other that we get in sync and flow together. I love that wild dancing feeling too, Honey. But you got so caught up in your story you forgot the topic. We are talking about the eyes of love. I want to share more about that now. (Michael laughs and nods his head, yes)

You and I have discussed this idea a hundred times over the years and it has come to be a really important concept for me. Not just because it is a lovely idea but because it actually is real. I do see you, the beautiful you, and I love that person and I can often see how you react to my vision of who you are and can be. You get inspired by it and you live up to it and I think my love for you and the way I see you is a big part of that."

Michael nods in agreement and picks up the conversation.

"Thanks, Sweetheart. I do want to comment more about this idea. I am convinced that the difficulty for many people is that we don't trust the way our lover sees us when we fall in love. That phrase 'love is blind' is part of the problem. Love is not blind. The truth is actually just the opposite. Love, this sort of love, gives us the ability to see another individual in all their glory and beauty. I remember the statement in the

Bible by the Apostle Paul when he said '*Now I see through a glass darkly but the face to face: now I know in part but then I shall know even as I am also known*'. Yes, I know he was not referring to romantic love. He was talking about a relationship with God, but I think his words can also apply to what happens to us when romantic love takes over our hearts. Before it shows up we cannot see the other person for who they truly are but this love gives us the sight to know, really know, our Beloved and that makes all the difference.

I see you, Dianna, and you see me, in a way no one has ever seen either of us. It is not a fantasy and it is not a form of intoxication. Our minds are not poisoned by love. To even think that is absurd and yet so many people fall prey to that ridiculous idea. I see you, Sweetheart! I see the real you and you are absolutely beautiful. I know you see me the same way. When that occurs we are both given a tremendously wonderful gift. Maybe it is the greatest gift one person can give another; to see them as so beautiful. I think every person who ever lived yearns for that precious experience; to be truly seen by another person. It is a completely validating event.

Once we are seen this way, we are changed. We do not forget it, ever. And, if that way of being seen is sustained, we begin to grow into that image. We actually fill it out and live up to it and that causes us to be even more grateful for our Beloved because she gave us the gift of becoming the best that we are.

Now, I just want to clarify one more thing if I can. (Dianna nods her agreement) That special and wonderful being that we see through the eyes of love is not a blueprint, it is the real person that, in a sense, lives in hiding in us behind our negative self-image that so often dominates our self-perception. This negative picture of who we think we are is the true imposter that has fooled us all our lives. Suddenly, with no warning, someone shows up and looks right through that crap and sees our real

117

being, and everything changes. I know this is what happened to us, Honey, and I am so grateful for you and how you see me every single day. You feel the same don't you?"

Dianna responds with enthusiasm.

"Yes, Sweetheart, I love how you see me. At first I had a hard time with it. I never thought of myself that way. I mean you see me as so special and precious and that felt good but also it felt strange. But then two things happened and keep happening and they help a lot. You are consistent in your wonderful perception of me, and I see you the same way. It helps a lot that I see you that way because I think it helps me accept your vision of me. I want you to accept how I see you as real, as valid. I love it when you do that, so it makes sense that you would feel the same way. My gift to you is to respect how you see me through the eyes of love. You offer me the same gift. That is how I see all this."

Michael hugs Dianna and voices his approval.

"Honey, you said it the best! That was it, all in a few words. Thanks! You are great!

Chapter 37

Seeing with the Eyes of Love: A Meditation

Imagine smog. Dense and grey and so thick you can see only a few feet ahead and behind. Imagine this is all you have ever known. For you it is not strange nor is it a problem. It is what it is and has always been. You move, day after smoggy day, through your life without a thought or expectation of anything bright appearing and never of any clear and brilliant horizon. Smog is what you know and grey is the color of yesterday, today and for all days to come.

Then for no reason you can discern, a hard rain falls. So hard it drives you to your knees. In moments, you are soaked, head to toe and then, just as suddenly, the rain stops.

Silence. Only the gentle sound of drops falling into puddles. You realize you have been kneeling with your eyes closed. You open them and first you can only see the wet grass at your knees. Something is different. Something has changed. The green is vibrant, shimmering and so intense you squint to protect your eyes.

Then you lift your head. It is a lifting and a seeing that will change you forever. One simple moment and movement, a brief and natural shift of muscle and bone and body and you are not the being you were before. You were a creature of the smog and now light penetrates you so deeply you fear you might break in pieces. Then just as quickly the fear falls away and you become an eye. Your body disappears and seeing is everything.

You see and see and see and colors burst against you without mercy and joy explodes in you, around you and before you. Everything is seeing and everything says hello and the tiny, plodding world of grey and smog is gone forever and you can see, and...you...can...see!

This is a brief and rather inadequate metaphor of what it is like to be suddenly given the eyes of love. Before these blessed eyes are grafted by grace into your heart you only see smog people, grey, plodding and far from magnificent. Then true seeing occurs and you look up from your knees into the face of one who is so radiant you forget to breathe.

Chapter 38

Affirmation is the Order of the Day

Between lovers, words matter. Loving words matter most. Romantic love grows wonderfully on loving words. It is essential that lovers learn to affirm each other as a normal and regular part of their daily communication. Noticing and then speaking clearly and directly about what is good, positive, special, valuable, endearing, fun, inspiring, sweet, caring, generous, wonderful, beautiful and lovable about one's partner is a learnable skill. It does not matter if either of you grew up in families that taught you how to do this. Most of us did not. Most of us have to learn this. The good news is that we can do it if we value it.

We cannot assume that our lover knows what we love and appreciate about them. In fact, we should assume that if they are not told then they don't know. Research, about couples who have sustained their loving romance for years, shows that they communicate positive information about and to each other at an approximate 10 to 1 ratio. Some couples say they do it at a 100 to 1 ratio. The second ratio is probably more accurate for couples who say they remain as much in love as they were when they met. It is important to note that being in love generates a desire to speak lovingly to one's partner and that speaking lovingly to one's partner nurtures the feeling of being in love. The energy and the feelings go both ways. The point, regardless of the numbers, is to create an atmosphere of consistent love and appreciation and the words we use contribute enormously to that.

Paying attention to what is positive about our partner increases our ability to see the positive. It does not invent positive by creating something that is not there. It simply enhances our ability to see what is present and real. If, however, we give our attention to the negative, then we will become expert on what is wrong with our lover and our feelings will follow. Negative begets negative and positive begets positive. Lovers who want to sustain and grow the wonder and ecstasy of romantic love will become expert on what is right and great about their partner and even more expert at communicating it. The results are usually immediate and wonderful.

It is important to note here that once either partner makes an effort to communicate what is positive, it is extremely important that the receiving partner do her or his part to take it in and allow the message to have an appropriate effect. If a lover sends a loving message and the partner deflects or belittles it, then the communication is blocked and the sender may hesitate to continue. It is crucial that the receiver learn to receive affirmation as if it is a precious gift from her or his partner. Then the receiving becomes as valuable as the giving. An appreciative reception of affirmation both invites and encourages the giving partner to continue offering love and care because the gift has been wonderfully acknowledged.

Chapter 39

Dianna and Michael – Affirmation

Dianna indicates that she wants to speak first.

"I like to think of myself as a positive person who sees what is good in others, but I have never experienced what Michael and I have created in our relationship in regards to positive communication. I really don't know who started it but we began affirming each other almost immediately and it has remained constant and equal. We both share what we love and enjoy and appreciate about each other every day. In fact (she laughs) just recently we talked about how great we are at being positive together. We laughed that we were being positive about how we are positive! It was funny but it is also really true. We have become amazingly good at it. And I love it. I love telling him and I also love hearing what he says to me."

Michael is smiling also and begins to share.

"Dianna is right. I think we were both inclined to voice our appreciation for each other from the moment we fell in love. It felt really good to me. I loved telling her what I loved and liked about her and how grateful I was for her and our relationship. I was a little afraid at first that she might feel it was too much, too intense, but she responded with enthusiasm. That seemed to inspire me to do it even more. I also realized really quickly that she peppered our conversation with positives and thank-you's and validation. I had never met anyone who was like that and I soaked it up. It made me want to be more of whatever she was affirming.

"I think it is important to say that neither of us grew up in families that did this. We have discussed this at length and are very clear about it. We had to learn how to affirm others and each other. It was not something we watched or heard or learned growing up. I think most people are like us. Few families teach their children how to notice the positive and affirm each other on any regular basis. So when those children become adults and fall in love they don't know how to voice their appreciation or approval of their lover. They may feel it in their hearts but they don't share it out loud and the relationship suffers from that and the love shrinks instead of expanding. I vowed never to let that happen between Dianna and me. I want her to feel wonderfully loved every single day we are alive together. Every day, no exceptions, so I tell her what I feel in my heart and she does the same with me, and it makes something truly incredible blossom between us."

Dianna nods in agreement and adds a comment.

"The last thing Michael said is so important. He said he vowed to keep our relationship special every day. He really meant that. He never takes what we have for granted and he treats me and what we have as precious. I suppose there are other men like that but I never met one. He is very special that way and his commitment makes me want to be the same.

"I also agree with him about having to learn to notice and speak positive things to one's partner. It can be too easy to notice but not say and then it turns into not noticing and the relationship goes downhill after that, especially the passionate part. The strange thing is that it is so easy with a little practice. Being in love sensitizes us to what is wonderful and special about our partner. We are intensely aware of it at the beginning but if we don't continue to verbalize it we lose touch and then the negative seems to rise to the forefront. Focusing on what is negative about our partner will really kill passion and that is a terrible loss. I hope we always have our passion and I want to do my part to make sure it stays alive. One of the best ways is simply paying attention to what is positive and wonderful about each other and sharing it with an open heart. Wow! That is powerful!"

Chapter 40

Death and Potential Loss are Real and Acknowledged

Very little makes us more aware of the preciousness of the present moment and the value of a loving relationship than the prospect of death. American culture pays almost no attention to the possibility of loss and as a result most couples also avoid the topic and its reality. The denial of death can protect us from uncomfortable thoughts and emotions, of course, but it also cheats us of a powerful technique for increasing the intensity of our romantic love. This notion may sound strange and even inappropriate at first hearing, but a deeper exploration can actually contribute to a heightened sense of aliveness and an intensified appreciation for the preciousness of each moment we have with our lover.

It is the child in us that imagines that all things live forever, and for children this idea is appropriate. Adults, however, are individuals who are fully aware that everything, animate and inanimate, has a beginning and an end and this includes human beings. This also includes lovers and as sad or terrifying that may seem, it is a fact. We can run from this awareness and live in denial or we can face its truth and learn to benefit from its potential blessing.

Yes, an acute awareness of the reality and possibility of death has a potential blessing. It is a blessing that equals the tragedy of death and prepares us for its coming. Thinking about death need not be morbid and dark, if we approach it with the proper attitude. Approached properly, it can aid us tremendously in feeling fully alive. It can help us value each moment this life brings us with our lover. Each touch becomes more special. Each word and laugh ring deeper into our being. Each smile radiates a light we may have missed if we were not paying such close attention. Every sexual encounter assumes a sacred quality that is both vibrantly sensual and mysteriously divine. Ecstasy, so rare in ordinary life, becomes a daily experience in our time with our lover. Each of these and all of these are part of the blessing of an awareness of the intimate presence of death in our life and love. It is up to us to find the courage to allow and engage it. Its gifts are worth getting past the fear.

Chapter 41

Dianna and Michael - Death

Dianna volunteers to speak first.

"I want to speak to this issue first because it will be hard to get Michael to stop once he starts. (She smiles at Michael and continues) I never liked to talk about death before I met Michael. I guess I was like most Americans who would rather leave it alone and get on with the business of my life. Death has not been a stranger to me, however. It shoved its ugly head into my life in a terribly painful way when I was in my early twenties. But I faced it and kept going and have mostly tried to accept that it is real but not give it more attention than I had to.

"Then Michael showed up and I fell completely in love with him and he started talking about death almost immediately. I thought, at first, that he was a little nuts. Actually, I still think that sometimes. (More laughter from both Dianna and Michael). But his nuttiness is attractive to me, including his persistence in talking about death on a regular basis. Over time and many discussions, it became clear to me that thinking about death could be something more than morbid. It has a purpose; at least it can have a purpose, if it is used the right way. Michael and I use it to keep ourselves from taking each other for granted. That is no small thing. Taking one's lover for granted is the beginning of the end for romantic love. It makes the mystery go away. It also takes away the feeling of gratefulness and, boy will that kill the special feeling we have! I would hate it if I stopped feeling grateful for him. If I have to bring up the possibility of my death or his death every once in a while to help me hang on to the mystery and gratefulness then OK. Done. I will do it, because it does help. It makes me really aware of how precious he is and we are together and that is an incredibly wonderful feeling.

She sighs in relief and motions to Michael that it is his turn.

"Dianna said it well and I guess we could stop there. (He looks for a moment as if he is finished and then he laughs and continues.) But, I do have a couple of things to add. Every time I think seriously about death one of Rumi's stories comes to mind. Please indulge me for a moment. I have to relate it.

"Rumi says that once a man named Nasrudin went to visit Father Abraham. Father Abraham was the Abraham of the Bible and was a very holy man. As they sat together talking in Father Abraham's tent, Nasrudin happened to look out the opening and saw the Angel of Death coming toward them. He immediately went into a panic and told Father Abraham that he was so afraid that he had to leave and go far way so that Death would not take him. He decided to run to China and quickly ran out the back opening and headed to the far away land of China. Very soon after Nasrudin's hasty departure, the Angel of Death arrived and sat down with Father Abraham. After they had spoken a while about deep and meaningful matters, the Angel asked Father Abraham if Nasrudin was the figure he had seen running out the back of the tent. Abraham nodded yes and the Angel of Death replied, 'I wonder what he is doing here. I am supposed to meet him in China.'

"I love that story. It is really funny and at the same time that it makes me laugh, it drives home a powerful point. We cannot run away from death. Even if we don't believe that we all have an appointed time to die, as this story implies, we will meet him someday no matter what. If that is true then it would be a wise thing to remember and live with that awareness and allow it to make each moment precious. That thought, that I take so seriously, that I never know if it is to be the last moment we have, makes my time with Dianna very, very precious. We may have 20 or 30 or more years together or just this day. I have no guarantee. So, my thinking about death will help me make today or this month or many years, special and precious with her. I don't want to miss a second of it. Not one."

Chapter 42

Forgiveness

Forgiveness is a commonly used but most frequently misunderstood spiritual and psychological concept. Most people think of forgiveness as something that lets the perpetrator off the hook without consequences for their hurtful act. This rather simplistic view of forgiveness appears to have no benefit for the hurt or harmed person. From his or her point of view, then, there is no clear reason or motivation to forgive. If this is the operable definition of true forgiveness then few of us will consider it even for the one we love the most.

What is needed, however, is not a rejection of forgiveness but a more developed definition and description of what it actually does for both the perpetrator and the victim. In Christian theology, forgiveness, as taught by Jesus, is a free gift of grace that heals both the perpetrator and the victim. He advised his followers to forgive 70 times 7, a number so large that it made it clear that one should let go of counting and make forgiveness a way of life. This radical directive was and is designed to change the lives and relationships of both the wounder and the wounded. It not only frees the perpetrator from guilt and shame and instills a sense of gratefulness, it also releases the one harmed, from anger, resentment and hatred. Finally, it clears the blockages between the two parties and makes a new relationship possible. This then is the deeper meaning of forgiveness that applies so powerfully to romantic lovers.

Every couple eventually has difficulties and in the midst of stress, one or the other will accidently or on purpose hurt the other. Tempers may flare and hurtful words and actions may fly and suddenly one or both are wounded. Once a wound occurs, whatever the depth, it is crucial for both lovers to quickly remember how precious their relationship is and act to heal the rift. It is the memory of and commitment to the ultimate value of their love for each other that will provide the strength to move toward forgiveness rather than disconnection and more hurt. This remembrance requires maturity and a willingness to make love more important than ego. Being immature and self-righteously right at these moments will block the process of healing and widen the gap between both partners.

The key to healing hurt between lovers is a shared commitment to hold their love as primary and make forgiveness a first choice when harm occurs. This decision is akin to building a house of love and placing a fire extinguisher (forgiveness) in every room. It is a form of wise preparation that will protect their home from any and all nasty sparks that suddenly appear. Forgiveness is then both a protection and a gift that a loving couple give themselves to ensure the strength and longevity of their relationship.

Chapter 43

Dianna and Michael - Forgiveness

Michael asks Dianna to speak first and she agrees.

"Michael, you and I have talked a lot about forgiveness and I think we both know that the idea that it is only for the forgiven is a big misunderstanding of what it is truly about. It seems that every religion teaches the value of forgiveness and I think there is a powerful reason for that. We need it to function as people in general and especially in an intimate relationship. We all get hurt at one time or another. I hurt you and you hurt me even though we try really hard not to. I am not saying, Honey, that we do it a lot. You and I are very careful not to hurt each other but it happens. When it does it is good to know that the other person wants to forgive even when the hurt is still being felt. I know you feel that way and I do also. It makes us partners in love. It is a strength we share and a commitment we both value."

Michael smiles and shares his response.

"Sweetheart, I like the way you said that. Yes, we are partners in love and forgiveness is something we both want and need to do for each other. It actually is a gift and a blessing. I think forgiveness is also an act of surrender. If you hurt me and I forgive you, I have to surrender my ego and sense of pride to do it. I have to get off my ego-generated high horse of, "I am right and you are wrong and you must feel the consequences of my upset." In the service of our love, it does not matter if I am right about how wrong you are. If we are going to heal and grow and continue on our path of love then forgiveness has to be a ready option no matter what. Do you agree with me?"

Dianna responds quickly.

"Yes, Sweetheart, I do agree. We need to have forgiveness as a ready option as you said. It really is a fire extinguisher and we need to use it as soon as possible when the sparks fly. The thought of this makes me feel safe with you. It means that I could make a mistake and know that you are committed to forgiving me. It does not make me feel as if I can get away with anything. I feel safe but not irresponsible. In fact, I feel even more responsible to treat you well because I know you have that commitment."

Chapter 44

Tolerating Love

Imagine that you have a vessel inside you that is designed to hold love. All the love that comes to you must fit into that container. If you receive more love than this vessel will hold all the excess love will drop away and be lost to you. How large is your vessel?

If your vessel is quart sized then what happens if life wants to shower you with a gallon of love? Is your vessel large enough to sustain your need for love? Who decided how large your vessel could be?

This exercise offers us information that is directly related to our ability to receive and tolerate love, especially romantic love. Many who do this exercise realize that the love-vessel inside of them is rather small. When romantic love showers down upon them unannounced, they accept what they can. However, if the power and intensity of it is greater than the vessel within them then they begin to deflect everything that seems more than they can handle. Romantic love is notoriously immense. It permeates our being with intense passion that is unlike anything we have ever experienced. In many cases it overwhelms our interior love-vessel to the point of overflow or even breaking. If we hold too tightly to the attitudes and beliefs that form and limit our ability to tolerate love, we will not be able to increase the size of our vessel and we will begin to shrink from the flow of love.

Much of today's self-help psychology emphasizes the importance of self-esteem and the difficulties that can arise due to the lack of it. Low self-esteem is blamed for many mental and emotional ailments, including a difficulty in tolerating affection and love. We might say that low self-esteem is a major factor in deciding the size of our interior love-vessel. Self-esteem generates our sense of what we believe we deserve. If then, we encounter a person who loves us more than we think we deserve, we could easily find ways to deflect or even reject some or all of that loving care and attention. Given the special intensity of romantic love, this could result in an enormous internal conflict between the limited size of our love-vessel and the enormity of the passion of our lover.

The miracle of romantic love, however, is its ability to re-shape and expand our interior love-vessel...if we consciously allow it. Currently, there are only three ways to substantially increase our ability to tolerate love; psychotherapy, which can take years and great financial expense; a transformational spiritual experience, which can occur gradually over years or in a lightning strike of divine intervention, which is not in our control; or finally by surrendering to the power of romantic love when it graces us with its joy. Both psychotherapy and spirituality are viable paths to self-love and it is true that loving God can include many of the experiences of romantic love, depending on the spiritual tradition. But this work is about romantic love and it appears we would do well to pay attention to its life and self-transforming powers.

It would be safe to assume that romantic love overwhelms everyone's love-vessel. For most of us, it is greater than any love we have experienced and our inner being is most often not prepared to fully accept and integrate it. Our task, then, is not to take what we can handle and let the rest fall away into the abyss of our self-hate. Our task is to muster all our strength and consciousness and open our heart to receive it until we think we are going to shatter internally and then open even more. The best and most effective response to romantic love is surrender. To surrender, in this instance, is not a sign of weakness. In fact, it is the opposite of weakness. It is actually an act of love responding to love with the only appropriate means we have. Heart must surrender to heart with a full sense of gratefulness. As we respond to love with love our inner vessel grows and expands until it can accept and hold the entirety of the miraculous gift is has been offered.

Surrendering to love is the best antidote to low self-esteem and all forms of self-hate. Surrender allows us to bypass the inner argument between our limited self-image and the glorious wonder that romantic love offers us. Rational defenses will not suffice. We cannot argue our way into believing that we deserve this immense blessing that has been bestowed upon us without our effort or request. We know, in our hearts, that we did nothing to earn it. Yet here it is, and it is our task to honor it by letting go of all resistance. Then love can enter every dark corner of our being and heal what we believed was unredeemable. At this point the inner love-vessel shatters completely and love fills all that we are. We are, once and for all, the vessel itself.

Chapter 45

Dianna and Michael- Tolerating Love

Michael holds Dianna's hand and begins to share.

"I used to think that the very idea of tolerating love was an absurd thought. It seemed to me that love was so wonderful that I would want all that I could get. It was sort of like that saying that you cannot be too skinny or too rich. The truth is, all three ideas are naïve at best and really dangerous at worst. I know the statistics about the majority of individuals who win the lottery. Suddenly they have millions of dollars and they think life will be stupendous and then two years later they say their life has never been worse. The truth I came to see is that people cannot hold on to wealth if they believe, deep down, they don't deserve it. Give a guy who is accustomed to earning $50,000 a year, fifty million dollars and he has no place to put it in his inner being and, my friends, inner being rules. It Rules! He does everything he can to trash it and very quickly, his external world and bank account equal his inner vessel for wealth. Ouch!

"I have seen the same thing with people who fall in love with a person they think is wonderful and special. Actually, romantic love makes everyone feel this way. They feel as if they have won the love lottery. Then, very soon, the old inner love-vessel takes over and it cannot take all that attention and tenderness, and care and real love making and bliss and joy and ecstasy. It is just too tiny to handle it and so a lover's heart begins to shut down and he pulls back from his partner and he says a couple of nasty things and she gets hurt and responds with the same and the whole thing begins a downhill slide into what so many sadly call normal life. The passion is gone and the love withers and boredom appears where mystery used to be. It makes me sick! Really sick, because it does not have to be that way."

Dianna holds her hand up and asks Michael to let her speak.

"Honey, I feel the same way. It is really sad when people fall in love and then lose it so quickly, especially when they could hold on to its joy or even make it better. I like what you said about winning the lottery a lot. That seems totally correct to me. I have had a couple of friends who fell in love and thought it was the best thing they ever experienced and then, less than a year later, they were bickering and bitching at each other like two little kids and the romance was nowhere to be found. I really don't want us to be that way, Sweetheart. I want our love to continue to grow and deepen and stay as special as it is now. I want to always be able and willing to receive all the love you give to me. If I ever start to feel that I am closing down from feeling overwhelmed by your love I will be sure to talk with you about it and try my best to open my heart again."

Michael looks at her with a large smile and nods enthusiastically.

"Sweetheart, the truth is you are the best love receiver I ever met. You are like a tenth degree black belt master at it. You are incredible at taking in my love and I can be pretty intense at times. You never hesitate. You never deflect and you never seem to go into denial. I am so grateful for that. My love is the best and most precious gift I have to offer and you always respond with an open and loving heart. I love you even more every time this happens. Something deep inside me has always wanted to love someone who would fully receive it and you are as close to perfect as I can imagine. I have no idea how you came to be this great at receiving love but I will be eternally grateful to you for it. You could give me no greater gift than that!"

Dianna responds quickly.

"Honey, it makes me so happy you feel this way. Your love is precious to me and I want it to fill my heart all the time. Nothing is better than that for me also. And, yes, Honey, you are wonderfully passionate and demonstrative and I love it when you are that way. I have never once felt you were too much for me. You are really good at responding to my love also, Sweetheart. I feel the same as you do. You never duck when I send my love or affection to you. I think I would get very hurt and disappointed if you did. But you don't let me down either."

Michael indicates he wants to add something.

"Honey, I want to say something more about that. I think falling in love makes everyone want to share their love without hesitation and everyone wants that love to be received with as much enthusiasm as it is being given. When that does not occur, I think the sender usually feels hurt and disappointed and that is often the beginning of the difficulties.

If I open my heart and offer you the very best thing I have to give, my love, and it is not properly received, what am I to do? Most people withdraw and withdrawal causes a disconnect. Sadly most couples don't know what to do when that disconnect occurs. They don't know how to repair the damage and then they simply learn to live with the distance. Emotional distance is not the friend of romantic love. It thrives on open hearted, vulnerable love sharing. I wish more couples discovered this truth before they lost their glow for each other."

Chapter 46

Habituation

Habituation is both a common and major contributor to the decline of romantic feelings in a loving relationship. It is defined as a decrease in response to a stimulus after repeated presentations. It occurs when two individuals fall in love and spend more and more time together. This may mean seeing each other daily, moving in together or getting married. In many ways it can be seen as a natural and inevitable part of a new relationship. If we fall in love, we naturally want to spend more time with our partner, and it thus appears that habituation and its effects on the intensity of our passion is unavoidable.

Habituation is caused by consistent repetition. It could mean eating the same thing for breakfast every day, or always wearing the same clothes to bed, or telling the same stories about friends, family or co-workers over and over, or watching the same TV shows each week, or ordering the same food at the same restaurant every time you eat out, or never eating out, or always having sex in the same position or the same day of the week, or becoming highly predictable in any way of thinking, talking, acting or emoting. Predictability is the natural result of habituation and predictability, in a loving relationship, usually produces boredom. Boredom, in a very real sense, is the opposite of romantic love. The more we become bored with our partner, the more quickly the intensity and frequency of our passion dissipates. Sadly, the great majority of couples succumb, without question or challenge, to this unfortunate situation. Then habituation wins the day and the couple loses its mystery and magic.

Habituation, however, is not inevitable and does not need to define the future years of a couple. It has an antidote that has the power to save or revive the joys of romantic love…if it is properly applied. The antidote is fourfold. It is a combination of spontaneity, gratefulness, mystery and savoring. Couples who value the wonderfully intimate, joy filled and often ecstatic experience of romantic love can learn to include and integrate each of these powerful ingredients into their relationship. Even a small effort usually has meaningful results and a large effort can create a renewal that is astounding.

To get an accurate idea of spontaneity think of being natural, informal, irreverent, unpredictable, impromptu, extemporaneous, and without constraint. When one is spontaneous, she or he has a sense of flow and surprise and even joy. Spontaneity is often contagious and invites others, especially our lover, to let go of formalities and be their more authentic selves.

Gratefulness, in this context, means to focus so clearly on what is positive and wonderful about one's partner that one feels full of gratefulness that they are alive and in one's life. We usually feel grateful for our lover when we consciously remember why we fell in love. The cultivation of gratefulness in a relationship can revive one's ability to enjoy being with one's lover. Noticing what we are grateful for and voicing it to our lover and to others will compound our sense of thankfulness for their love and very being.

Savoring means to relish, to enjoy and to appreciate something or someone, especially our lover. It is closely related to being grateful and can be used in conjunction with it. To savor requires what might be called mindfulness, a choice to pay real and full attention to what we are doing and/or feeling at any given moment. To savor our lover means that we stop our minds and busyness and allow our hearts to soak in his or her beauty. This usually produces an intense experience of excitement and appreciation of our partner.

Mystery is by definition a bit more difficult to define. However, it implies that each partner is not fully known or understood by the other. Mystery disappears when we imagine or assume we know all there is to know about our lover. Mystery appears when we realize that our lover is complex and not completely predictable or knowable. Mystery has a quality of surprise and a sense that there is always something more to this person we love.

When we combine all four of these qualities and practice them regularly, habituation shrinks and romantic love blossoms. Initially, it may take some effort to attend to and develop each one. Learning new behavior can be difficult but the health and vigor of your romance will more than repay any awkwardness that occurs at the start. Then, with practice, each of these qualities will become a blessing to you and your lover and you will become an inspiration to everyone who knows you.

Chapter 47

Dianna and Michael - Habituation

Michael has quite a bit of energy about this subject and he begins the conversation.

"I know this might sound strange but I love this word, habituation. I like the way it sounds. Yes, it would be easy to say it means doing something over and over until you lose awareness of it, but the word is cool. I also like the idea, at least I like its message, because it is so important for couples who want to keep their sense of romance. Habits of any kind generate desensitization and that leads to a loss in intensity in a relationship.'

Dianna speaks up.

"Honey, I know you are correct but you might be a little too intellectual here. I know you like the word but let's talk a little more about how we prevent it in our relationship. Actually you are amazingly good at it. (Michael smiles and Dianna continues) You find a thousand ways to do all four of those things that couples are supposed to do to keep the romantic feeling alive. You inspire me, Sweetheart, and I have learned to do the same thing."

Michael jumps back in the conversation.

"Yes, you really can be spontaneous yourself and I love it. I especially love it when you sing in the middle of lovemaking. (Michael laughs and Dianna blushes) Wow! You don't do it every time and so it always surprises me but it is such a spontaneous and beautiful thing that you do. And, no, I am not going to share anything else that personal about our sex life. At least not now! (He laughs again and Dianna punches him playfully in the side) Ouch! I promise.

"I also love it when you dance in the aisles at the grocery store. Someday I hope I am relaxed enough to dance with you. I think everyone who sees you do it loves it also. Actually, now that I am thinking about this, you do spontaneous dancing just about everywhere. You dance in the grocery store, you really go at it in the car with the music pumped up, on the street and in the house. I could go on about this but you get the point. I love to watch how gracefully and sensually you move. You seem so free and joyful and you make my heart fill up when you do that. There is a Yiddish word for this experience called *kvelling*. It means to look with loving eyes at someone and fill up with gratefulness for their existence. You cause that to happen in my heart a lot."

Dianna raises her hand for a pause and then begins to share.

"OK, Honey, I get it and I love that you love me that way. I have a few things to add about you also. You are always full of surprises that are happy, quirky and often very loving. You frequently surprise me with a little gift, like a zip bag of my favorite coffee that you ground for me or two big bottles of apple juice from the wholesale warehouse. You might text me with a link to a song that reminds you of us or me or write a poem about the inside of my elbow (see above). And you are the best at savoring. This one is really special to me. I love it when you stop and simply look at me with your full attention and it feels as if you are memorizing my face or my hand. I feel so in love with you when you do that. It is a precious moment for me and it makes me want to do the same with you. It has always been clear that you are fully committed to keeping our love alive and you do lots of things every single day that help us stay excited about each other. I am so blessed that you are that way!"

Michael is deeply touched by what Dianna has shared and he speaks very softly as he responds.

"Sweetheart, you have always been the best at doing affirmations. You include them in so many of our communications, on the phone and texting and in person. You do it so well I often feel like a puppy wagging his tail and rolling over and over in his enthusiasm when you do that. I know that might sound a bit silly but I really feel that way a lot when you are with me. It makes me want to be better and better at all the things that make our love grow.

"The part about mystery is particularly interesting to me. People who live together for some time often feel they know pretty much everything about their partner. I believe that making that assumption is both erroneous and dangerous. The truth is we can never know everything about another person. No one is the same today as yesterday and not one of us can see into the depths of another and know all that is there. Any time one lover decides he or she knows the other completely then the real person disappears and a static image takes their place. Then surprise cannot occur and boredom begins. I never want you to become bored with me. I want to be continually growing and changing in ways that make me more interesting and lovable and desirable to you. I want to be that way until the moment just before this life is over. It is a basic ingredient in being fully alive and I want to be alive with you every day."

Dianna puts her hand on his arm and nods in agreement and shares with the same enthusiasm.

"Honey, you just did what I love. You got so excited about what we were talking about that you became inspiring to me and now we have to get a room! (She laughs and Michael laughs also). OK, the room can wait but I mean it. You live what you preach, Honey, and that is a giant turn on for me. I could eat you up!"

Chapter 48

Creating a Safe Space

Every individual needs safety in order to prosper and grow and have a meaningful sense of well being. This safety must begin with physical safety but must also include emotional, mental and spiritual safety as well. Romantic love is no exception. Both lovers must create and maintain a safe space for each other. This means, of course, that physical force and/or violence must never be part of the relationship. It also means that each lover must respect the personal boundaries of the other at all levels. This could mean anything from being nonjudgmental of the other's feelings, thoughts and behavior to refraining from looking at their email or cell phone messages. Each partner must have a feeling of safety in the presence of the other at all times. If this does not occur then each will begin to censor her or his sharing and this will immediately erode intimacy.

A healthy and robust romantic relationship should be the safest relationship that either partner has ever experienced. It is the one supreme place that each can expect to be accepted and loved. It is where facades and masks and all forms of phoniness can be dropped. It is a place that nurtures authenticity, vulnerability and radical honesty. It is a space without attack or shaming, judgment or ridicule. It is a holy place in which secrets can be told, confessions can be made and redemption is always available.

This aspect of romantic love is so essential and crucial that each partner must take on the task of protecting the safety of the other as a sacred responsibility. No safety will quickly equal no relationship. Therefore, any breach or violation of safety between lovers must be immediately attended to and healed. Otherwise, romantic love will dissipate and finally disappear.

Chapter 49

Dianna and Michael – A Safe Space

Dianna waves her hand and indicates she wants to start the discussion.

"I feel really safe with you, Honey, but I did not realize how important safety was until we began our relationship. I guess I never felt it with anyone the way I feel it with you. I never worry about being attacked or judged and especially being shamed and I would be totally shocked if you got physical with me, in a bad way I mean (she laughs). In my past relationships I never really worried about being hit but I did have to deal with judgment and ridicule. I hated that and I know we paid a terrible price for it. It truly destroys any desire to be close and it often creates a tendency to behave the same way. It surely did not bring out the best in me or my partner. Wow!, this safety thing is a big deal! I am so glad we are thoughtful about it."

Michael responds as soon as Dianna pauses.

"Honey, I completely agree with you. It does seem obvious that feeling safe is so important. Yet so many people grow up without it, and therefore don't expect it in their relationships, even with the person they are supposed to love the most of all. I think the love of my life, that's you, Baby, should be the person I feel safest with and you should feel the same about me. If I cannot feel safe with you, then what? What is love about if it is not about safety? It has to start there and stay there in order for everything else to develop. I need to feel safe with you in order to bare my soul with you and I want to bare my soul with you, Honey. It is a wonderful, healing and even transforming experience to be able to share my hurts and hopes and dreams and failures with you and not worry about rejection or some other form of negative reaction on your part. I love that and I love you for being so safe. I definitely want to be the same for you."

Chapter 50

Self-sacrifice

The United States is the world's icon for individualism. We have traditionally placed more emphasis on the individual than any other country in recorded history. We emphasize individual rights, responsibility and self-reliance and we strongly encourage the same values in any and all interaction we have with other countries. Being independent and self-reliant are useful and desirable characteristics, of course, but, like all other ideals, they have a shadow side. The dark side of individualism is narcissism, and sadly, we North Americans (USA) are arguably the most narcissistic country ever. We are the king, queen and royal court of selfies and no one is better than us at indulging in self-centered thinking and activities.

Everyone has some degree of narcissistic thinking but most people also have an ability to think outside of the Me-box and feel compassion and care for others. That ability is brought to center stage when we fall in love. Romantic love is the antithesis of narcissism. It draws us out of ourselves and invites us to lift our eyes from our own navels and become enthralled with the vision of an Other who is magnificent. We feel a powerful drive to make our partner happy without concern about our own needs or desires and we begin to feel the freedom of a healthy sacrifice of self in the process.

Romantic love, for many individuals, is their first encounter with healthy self-sacrifice. We actually feel compelled to attend to the needs of another person before we think of ourselves. Our lover's desires are suddenly paramount to us and we give great amounts of our time and energy to discovering and acting upon what makes that person happy. Then, thanks to the intensity and depth of our love, we actually feel exhilarated when they are pleased, whether or not our own needs are met.

This kind of dedication and willingness to please our lover can be a bit frightening to some. We, who are supposed to be so independent, may become uncomfortable at the thought of being too committed to giving so fully to another person. It may be seen as a loss of self, or worse, to the self-reliant devotee, a loss of independence. But, in the context of romantic love, it is not a loss but a gain. We gain a freedom we could not have imagined because it is far too large for the tiny Me-box we have heretofore inhabited. It is the freedom to think and feel passionately about something other than ourselves and to find intense joy in that process.

If, however, we are too stuck in our narcissistic independence, we will find romantic love increasingly threatening and will begin to create distance from our partner until the threat subsides. Sadly, that distance that seems so necessary for the protection of our personal boundaries will also limit our ability to enter into the sacred depths of radical intimacy. The loss of radical intimacy will then cheat us of the most valuable and life transforming possibilities of romantic love. The best choice, even if it is at first uncomfortable, is to surrender to the heart-driven desire to please our lover. The risk is worth the gift that it will produce. Anything less and we will miss the waiting treasure.

Chapter 51

Dianna and Michael – Self-sacrifice

Michael steps up and begins to speak first.

"This whole idea of self-sacrifice is so important. Letting go of one's agenda is what it is about most of the time. It is not really about losing a grasp of who one is or becoming co-dependent or your lover's servant. It means caring so much about the happiness and well-being of our partner that we are able to drop our ego and put them first. Most of the time that occurs in pretty ordinary ways. For example, if I am watching TV and you ask me to change a light bulb, I put the show on hold and handle the bulb. No problem. No fuss and no stress. I don't decide that you are trying to control me or that you are being inconsiderate of my needs. It was just a TV show and it is on hold. Now I know this could involve much more important decisions and issues such as where we live or whose family we visit on a holiday or what care we buy. Each of these situations could turn into a stressor for the average couple. Unless both partners were willing to do some self-sacrifice for the other. Then it becomes a matter of discussion rather than conflict and both end up happy."

Dianna indicates she has a contribution to make.

"Honey, I do agree with what you are saying. I think it works best when both partners have the same attitude. In fact, if only one has this attitude then the whole relationship will be out of balance pretty fast. Right? (Michael nods his agreement.) I always feel you are willing to give me what I want or need without argument or conflict, unless it seems not so good for me. I have the same attitude about you. We are so much that way that sometimes it is funny because we both want the other person to have what they want. And, to tell the truth, I never feel as if I am missing out or that I don't get my needs met because of you. I am so convinced that you want me to be happy that it makes me want to do the same for you. That is what creates the balance.

"Self-sacrifice has often seemed like a hard thing to me. Before we met, I thought of it as frequently painful and difficult. I saw it as giving up something that was important to me for another person and not necessarily getting anything back. But I have learned that it can be a wonderful way to relate almost daily with you. It makes me happy to let go and give to you. I know you feel the same way. Actually, most of the time it does not feel like sacrifice. There is very little if any suffering involved. I don't feel taken advantage of or manipulated or used. I feel joy at being able to give you what you want.

"I want to be very clear about this, Sweetheart. I am not trying to say either of us is perfect or saintly. Far from it. I am really saying that healthy mutual self-sacrifice in a loving relationship truly makes both lovers happy. It feels good. It feels good to both of us. So why not do it? I think of it as putting love-money in the bank. It makes lots of interest. That is about it!"

Chapter 52

Responsiveness

Of the many attitudes and behaviors that are essential to the sustenance of romantic love, responsiveness is one of the most central. When a lover offers her most precious gift, her heart, to another, the quality and depth of the response is crucial. A shallow, insensitive or partial response will break the flow of intimacy and often cause the sender to hesitate or withdraw. Sharing love, of the most intimate kind, requires vulnerability and vulnerability requires an open hearted reception followed by a giving back of love at the same level and intensity. The open hearted response of the one receiving love creates a new level of safety for the one who has shared. This act has divine qualities and effects because it can both validate and heal at the same moment.

We have no greater gift to offer another than our deepest, heart filled love. It is the most precious treasure that we possess. To drop all defenses and present the dearest part of our being to another requires both courage and devotion. How our partner responds to that offering will make all the difference for the future of who we will become together.

An impaired ability to respond to our partner's love offering will cause hurt, confusion and withdrawal and ultimately an end to all meaningful intimacy. An open and responsive heart will create an ever deepening flow of love that can last for a lifetime. Too often, one or both partners will exhibit an insensitivity to this truth, that responsiveness is essential. This could be based in immaturity, which means there is a lack of experience with intimate loving relationships. With the proper guidance this difficulty can be overcome and the couple can grow together in their ability to respond with care and sensitivity to one another. A more serious blockage to responsiveness can originate in childhood wounds that make an individual fearful about showing or receiving vulnerability. In these cases the wounded partner may withdraw or shutdown when his or her partner offers love. If this becomes a style of responding then it could require a professional to help the wounded one identify and heal the pain that blocks her or his ability to respond appropriately to loving intimacy.

Chapter 53

Dianna and Michael - Responsiveness

Michael hesitates and then asks Dianna to go first.

"Michael, I know you have quite a bit of passion about this subject so I think I will share first and then you can talk as long as you want, Honey. (Michael nods agreement and smiles at her.)

"I have a lot of experience with an unresponsive partner and it taught me at least two lessons. First, when I was affectionate and got a tiny reaction or worse, nothing at all, I felt small and insignificant and I wanted to shut down and go away. It made me wonder why I was in the relationship at all. So I eventually stopped showing affection and just did my own thing. We became like roommates instead of lovers.

We did not fight and I guess that was good but passion and closeness ceased to exist. Sadly, my experience taught me the importance of no response in a relationship and how it can cause complete shutdown and disconnection.

"The second lesson is very closely connected to the first. At first I thought my need for a supportive response to my affection was my problem. I was told that I was too needy and too emotional and for a while I actually believed it. But then I took a deeper look and talked to friends and a couple of professionals and I began to realize that healthy people have healthy needs and that I was not crazy. I wanted and needed to share my heart and have my partner share his. That is what intimate, romantic love is all about. I was not nuts or too needy. I was normal. When I accepted this truth about myself I felt sad for myself and my partner. We could not connect because he was too shutdown and, tragically, believed that he did not have a problem. This attitude made change or healing impossible for him and it completely closed the door between us."

Dianna becomes tearful and motions for Michael to continue the conversation.

"Sweetheart, I can see you feel some pain about that. If you want to say more just let me know. (She nods agreement and Michael continues.)

"You are the most love-responsive person I have ever known. I am very sad you had to go through that pain but it surely made you clear that being responsive is so important. Your responsiveness has really had a tremendous effect on me. Every time I share my love with you, you respond so beautifully that I want to love you even more. I feel accepted and valued and validated and blessed and so grateful, and my heart wants to open even more and pour all that I have out to you. (He smiles.) I am gushing, I know. I can't help it, Honey. Your ability to be exactly what I need you to be when I give you the best gift I have is incredible.

I think I knew intuitively that what you give me is what I have always wanted and needed but I never got it…until you. I have often said that your responsiveness to my affection and vulnerability is so special that I feel like a puppy who is wagging his tail so hard he might fall down.

"I know you might blush when you hear this but I truly think you are a master at being responsive to love. I have never met anyone better at it than you and in fact I have never met anyone who comes even close. I don't know what I did to deserve you but I am eternally grateful and I am also completely committed to responding to your love with as much care as you give me.

"I am convinced that our mutual responsiveness is a major factor in why our romance is still so intense. Each time I share my love with you, you respond wonderfully. You never ignore me or take me for granted or have the attitude that it is the same ole same ole stuff. I feel that deeply and I give the same back to you. It makes our love fresh and alive and often ecstatic. I love that! I really love it! I think it would break my heart if we ever stopped responding so lovingly to each other."

Dianna indicates that she agrees and begins to share again.

"Honey, you are so right about all of that. I just want to add that you also have the gift of responsiveness. I never have to worry that I might open my heart and my love would fall on insensitive ears with you. It also makes me want to do the same for you. And, yes, Sweetheart, I agree that being this way keeps us alive and fresh like it is the first few months of falling in love. I never, ever imagined that it could be this good for so long but it is, Honey and we are."

Chapter 54

Hold the Relationship as Precious

One of the most powerful ways to nurture and protect romantic love is for both partners to view their relationship as precious. Yet many couples, even those in love, treat their relationship as if it is plated in steel. They speak harshly and behave hurtfully to each other as a matter of course and then wonder why the initial glow dims so quickly. Romantic love, however, will not tolerate harsh treatment. This sort of intolerance is not a sign of weakness. It is actually an invitation to both lovers to join together in a new form of relatedness. This new way of being is best described as precious. To hold a relationship as precious means to see it as having great or enormous value. It also means that it must not be treated carelessly.

Romantic love comes to us as grace, meaning it is a free gift, and as such it should be held as precious. We are not careless with anything that is precious to us. We do not ignore the needs of something that is precious. We do not take it for granted and we do not handle it thoughtlessly. Instead we create a safe space for that precious thing and we give it our care-filled attention.

To consider romantic love as precious and to practice that daily in a relationship will produce a level of intimate interaction that is seldom seen in our culture. Every aspect of the lovers' connection will assume a heightened sensitivity that neither partner may have experienced in any other part of their lives. Ordinary events will become special and intensified. Walking the dog, shopping, cleaning house, watching TV, having dinner with family or friends, driving to work, all of these normal experiences will take on a new quality of tenderness and intimacy that will bring joy and even ecstasy. All of this will occur because lovers are committed to holding their relationship in a context of precious.

Chapter 55

Dianna and Michael - Precious

Dianna has quite a bit of energy about this topic and she speaks first.

"I love this word precious! It seems so right as applied to a romantic relationship, but before I met and fell in love with Michael, I had never heard it used this way. He began to describe our love as precious almost immediately. In fact, he used it over and over again and so I began to use it too. It is accurate. Our relationship, our love, this very special thing we have together is truly precious to both of us. Because we think of it this way then we treat it as such. We both try very hard to be thoughtful and full of care in how we interact. I think if we were Buddhists we might say we are mindful in our relationship, but mindful is not quite it. Yes, we pay attention to our connection and behavior but the word precious carries more weight and meaning than that. To call something or someone precious makes me want to treat that person with great care, with tenderness, with sensitivity. I would never want to be careless with something that is precious. Insensitive and careless and coarse and harsh are the opposite of how I relate to a precious person. It is a special word and it carries a special meaning. Calling our relationship precious is our way of acknowledging its enormous value, of course, but it also implies that it must be treated with extra care. Don't you agree, Michael?"

Michael smiles and nods in agreement.

"Absolutely, Sweetheart; you said it perfectly. I love the word also and like you, I had never heard it used to describe a romantic relationship, but it is exactly right for us and I think it is right for anyone who falls in love. Falling in love creates a precious relationship and it would be great if all lovers felt that way. When I use the word in reference to us it reminds me to interact with you with extra care, just as you said. That extra care has a very large effect on how we get along on a daily basis. In a real sense, it protects us from harming each other. If you and we are precious to me then I will be careful in how I speak to you. I don't mean to say that I censor or inhibit myself around you. Far from it. But I do remind myself that being tender is better than being rough or insensitive and being thoughtful is better than being careless.

"One of the best examples of this idea of holding our relationship as precious is that we never curse each other, either in anger or in jest. We just don't do it because we feel that what we have is too precious to bang it around with hard language. It is not that we don't use curse words. We do. You do particularly when someone cuts you off in traffic. (He laughs.) OK, I do too, Honey, and not only in that situation but in others. But I never curse at you. You are far too precious to me for that language, I don't care what happens. And the truth is, I am proud of me and us that we are that way. I am a person that is rarely shocked and I would probably fall on my face in shock if you cursed me. (He laughs again.) You know I am right, don't you?"

Dianna is laughing also and she responds.

"Yes, Sweetheart, I would think I did something terrible if you ever cursed me and I would feel really guilty if I spoke to you that way."

Michael indicates he wants to add something.

"I want to make this clear. You and I are not prudes. We are not prim and proper people and we are not uptight. This conversation about precious is not about that. It is about learning to see the real and significant value in romantic love. It is really, really, special and powerful and valuable and incredible and it is definitely precious. Anyone who does not see that has a sad and serious form of blindness. OK, that is the whole thing I want to say."

Chapter 56

Hold the Relationship as Sacred

Holding a relationship as sacred is closely related to the previous idea of holding it as precious. Not everything that is precious is sacred but everything sacred should, of course, be held as precious. To think of a relationship as sacred brings it into the realm of spirituality and it is here that we encounter the numinous quality of romantic love. Sacred implies something holy, blessed and venerated. Something that is sacred is related to the divine. In truth, we do not usually assign the quality of sacredness to romantic love. It is not a choice we make. It is part of the essence of love and especially this particular and special love that has the power to transform two lives.

We live in a culture in which little is held as sacred and because of that many romantically entwined couples do not think to consider it as such. This lack of awareness deprives them of access to many of the non-ordinary gifts of romantic love. It is like being given the key to a wonderful mansion but once inside never venturing beyond the living room. Yes, it might be more beautiful than any room one has ever seen, but that room is only one of many and that glorious space is only a sample of the wonders deeper in the mansion. Sadly, many lovers never discover the incredible treasures waiting further in that magnificent structure because they have little or no awareness of the real meaning of sacred.

When a couple becomes open to the sacred aspect of their relationship they become receptive to its spiritual qualities and possibilities. In common language, we might say they are now open to the presence of God in their love. Now they are able to see and feel that Presence and if they are truly wise, they will surrender to it with all their heart. To acknowledge the sacred quality of their love is to begin to know the Author of Love, the One who created this blessed gift and who now graces them with its treasure. It is the sacred power of love that lifts them out of the ordinary and mundane form of relatedness and transports them into higher and higher levels of passion and ecstasy. It is at these levels that inner healing can occur and an intimacy and experience of oneness that is beyond the capacity of speech.

Few couples reach these special places but only because they have not learned to hold their love as sacred and do not trust its power. The good news is that every couple blessed by the gift of romantic love has an invitation to enter this mansion and find the sacred gifts that await them. It is a matter of trust and choice. Even a little trust will accomplish great things.

Chapter 57

Dianna and Michael - Sacred

Dianna begins.

"I was raised in a religions that taught that marriage was sacred. I always thought that meant that the institution was what was sacred. The thing itself was what was important. I never really questioned that idea until Michael and I began our relationship. Yes, I still think of marriage that way but, for me, the real sacredness is the relationship. It is the coming together, the connection, the flow of love, that makes this sacred, not the official ceremony. Hearts sharing deep, trusting, passionate love create the sacred quality, the holiness, not a formality. Our love, that mysterious and powerful thing that hold us together is holy and it is very spiritual. We both feel closer to God in the midst of being closer with each other, and that experience can be extremely intense sometimes. (She pauses and looks at Michael) Honey, I know you agree with me. Can you share more about this?"

Michael nods a yes and continues the conversation in a quiet and serious tone.

"Thanks, Honey. I have a theory about this. Yes, our connection is both sacred and holy and I am convinced that that is what it is supposed to be. Romantic love is a uniquely special invitation and, yes, a path, to know what divine love is, to experience it in real time in real life. So many people have a hard time finding any true and life changing experience of God these days. They try all sorts of religions but come away empty or even disappointed but then this sort of love takes hold of them and they are transported to a level of passion and love that knocks their socks off. It is too bad someone does not tell them that this is God, this is divine energy, this is sacred territory and they have been chosen to receive it. But, I guess I am doing that right now and I hope lots of lovers will listen to this and pay attention. No, I am not selling religion. Yes, I am saying that something sacred is occurring here and that it is an incredible gift. It is a precious, sacred, holy and really, really life-changing gift. Treat it that way and it will be the best thing you have ever experienced."

Chapter 58

Maturity is Valued, Sought and Practiced in All Aspects of the Relationship

Sustaining a committed relationship, even when it is blessed with romantic love, requires two mature individuals. Immaturity will erode and eventually destroy even the most well intentioned couple's intimate connection. Romantic love is truly an adults-only event. It cannot be sustained by children or adolescents. It cannot last if one partner is mature and the other is immature. It takes two adults who are committed to interact, no matter what, with thoughtful maturity.

Sadly and unfortunately, many couples who fall in love do not have, nor do they seek adulthood. Individuals with adult bodies, act like teenagers (or even younger children) and then are shocked that love seems to be so difficult. In their immaturity, they expect love and lust to be enough and that it should last simply because it showed up. This naïve attitude might seem ridiculous but it is the culprit behind the destruction of many marriages that began with real and intense romantic love.

It is a strange fact that more training is required of an individual who seeks a driver's license than one who applies for a marriage license. We require more maturity of someone who wants to drive a car than one who is making the most complicated and life-changing commitment of her or his life. One could easily make an argument that 16 year olds are far too immature to be driving but no one seems to make the same argument about what level of maturity should be required for a marriage license.

Many couples' therapists will testify that immaturity is one of the most central factors in the success or failure of a marriage. Partners who act like children are the majority who populate the counseling rooms of professionals across the nation. Each partner has become an expert at blaming the other for their troubles and few are mature enough to take responsibility for her or his part in the difficulty that brought them to counseling. Blaming is childish and leads to hurt and disconnection. Resolution only becomes possible when both partners finds some modicum of maturity and relate as two caring adults.

Every couple blessed by the gift of romantic love, must commit themselves to the rigorous pursuit of adult attitudes and behaviors. This love can actually facilitate that growth if a couple is open to it. Romantic love can bring out the best in an individual and his or her partner and that best is always a path to being a better adult. The choice for adulthood must, however, be made daily, and sometimes moment to moment. The payoffs far outweigh the initial effort and it actually gets easier with practice.

Chapter 59

Dianna and Michael - Maturity

Dianna begins with a bit of hesitancy.

"This topic is hard for me because I sometimes worry if I am being adult enough. I want to be mature and I know how important it is but I know I am not perfect and I really hope I can be grown up most of the time, Honey."

Michael smiles And responds.

"Sweetheart, you are not only mature almost all the time but you help me with that issue. You encourage me to be patient, not over react, calm down before I respond and a hundred other things that relate to being mature. I try to be mature also, Honey, but I rely on you to support me that way and you never let me down.

"That phrase, "romantic love is truly an adults-only event" really hits me. It is right on. This thing we have is beautiful but it is also complex and sometimes difficult. It is not difficult because of you or even me but because life brings us difficult things to handle like family and money and work and children and a million other things and circumstances that require thoughtfulness and patience and cooperation, to name a few. We could never survive as lovers if we were insensitive, selfish, took things personally, overreact, had unrealistic expectations, and attacked each other when we were stressed. I could name at least a hundred different ways partners can be childish and every single one of them contributes to a blockage in partnership and intimacy and deep love.

"And one more thing. Real intimacy really requires maturity. Chidden and adolescents get giggly and uncomfortable when they see two people being emotionally intimate. They cannot handle it, and deep emotional intimacy is essential to a strong and lasting relationship of romantic love. There is no question about it. This love we have is truly adults-only. Any couple that tries to make it work without being adult is doomed to pain and ultimate failure."

Dianna indicates she has something to add.

"Honey, you are right. Being mature is crucial and, yes, I am a mature person. I know I am because I do my part when we are in the stressful situations that show up. We both support and encourage that sort of thinking and behavior in each other and that helps a lot. We are not perfect about it, of course, but both of us are quick to admit it when we have a lapse and get back on track before we do real damage. Oh, that reminds me of one more thing I wanted to add.

"Being able to admit when one is wrong is a truly important part of a successful romantic relationship and that is certainly an adult quality. I know so many people who have a difficult time admitting their mistakes and some who cannot do it at all. That difficulty is really common in teenagers but it should not be part of an adult loving relationship. It shuts the door when two people have a disagreement and makes it impossible to find resolution in so many circumstances. In truth, easily admitting that one is wrong, especially in relationship to one's partner, is a gift. It is also endearing and supportive. And, also important, it is loving because it is a form of selfless giving. When I say or you say, 'I was wrong about that' we are more interested in our relationship than we are in our own egos. That is something only a mature adult can do.

Michael quickly responds.

"Honey, you are good! I love that and I love you!"

Chapter 60

Words Matter...Always

As children, many of us learned a nursery rhyme to shout back at others who were taunting us. *"Sticks and stones may break my bones but words will never hurt me."* The rhyme never really worked because it is a lie. Words do hurt and in many cases they do terrible damage, especially between lovers. Lovers, by definition, are two individuals who have willfully dropped their defenses and opened their hearts to each other. Love lives on openness and all true lovers know this intuitively. A lover's words have special and powerful meaning to the beloved. They can lift and inspire and heal, and even transform. They can also cut to the bone. Between lovers there are no insignificant or throwaway words. All communication has meaning and consequences.

Romantic love has its own vocabulary and tone. Vocabulary means the actual words we use, such as Dear, Honey, Sweetheart, please and thank you. Tone has to do with the sound of the communication. A loving word can be delivered with a tender or sweet tone or it can sound harsh and grating. Used the first way, it will nurture and support the recipient. Used with a harsh tone, even a tender word like Sweetheart can hurt an undefended receiver. Many couples begin their relationship with attention to how they communicate. Their words and tone reflect caring and tenderness. Then, as they begin to merge (see section on merging and romantic love) they take each other more and more for granted and their style of communication deteriorates. Love language loses its dominance and a colder, less caring communication style takes over. Endearing words couched in sweet tones take a back seat to brusque utilitarian language and intimacy takes a beating.

Too many couples treat their words as insignificant and give little thought to their effects on their lover. But name calling, cursing, sarcasm, hurtful teasing, shaming, and belittling, combined with tones that communicate disdain, repulsion, judgment, derision, disrespect and general insensitivity, all quickly erode precious intimacy and romance. On the other hand, words that affirm, support, encourage, inspire, nurture and admire, couched in tones that are tender, sweet, caring and joyful create a symphony that enhances the dance of romance and wonderful closeness. The question is whether both partners are willing to give consistent attention to their communication and make sure that love language is the order of each interaction.

Chapter 61

Dianna and Michael – Words Matter

Dianna begins the conversation with an affirmation.

"Michael you are absolutely wonderful in your communication with me. You pay really close attention to how you speak to and with me and you have been an inspiration to me because of that."

Michael jumps in with a response.

"Dianna, you are actually an inspiration to me also. You have always talked to me with such care and tenderness that sometimes it makes me cry because I am so grateful. Your gentleness is so consistent and your tone is never, ever nasty even if you seem to be frustrated with me. You don't get frustrated with me a lot but I can be difficult sometimes, and you always handle me so lovingly that I melt and don't feel like getting defensive. That is amazing! You are amazing!"

Dianna responds with enthusiasm.

"Michael, you are doing exactly what I love right now. You are so affirming to me. You constantly tell me what you appreciate about me and you really want me to let it in. (She laughs) You will even tell me to take a breath and let in the love. I have learned to do that and your words mean even more to me because of it."

Michael is smiling and begins to share in response.

"Sweetheart, you know that words have always been important to me. I know a word can make a tremendous difference between two people and a word couched in the right tone can have an even more powerful affect. That is why I am never sarcastic with you. (He pauses and reflects) I don't want to sound professorial but sarcasm comes from a Greek word which means to tear flesh. Being sarcastic with someone we love is often a way to disguise anger and it hurts, and for sure does not make a couple closer.

"I think everything we say to each other matters. Our choice of words matter and our tone matters. I cannot say it with more conviction. I have come to love how we talk to each other. I often reflect on our conversation and how even the most ordinary communication can add to our love. I know this may sound strange but I enjoy how we talk to each other when we shop for groceries. We find a hundred ways to enjoy each other as we get bananas and onions and order meat in the deli and choose what milk we want to drink. We talk like lovers and we are funny and sweet and helpful and…I could go on and on about this but I think I have made my point. Most of our relationship is built around and on talking and how we do that can make it special and joyful, and we make sure that we choose joyful. Honey, we are really good at that!"

Dianna laughs and joins in.

"Honey, you are right. We do have a great time shopping and not only for groceries. We can do the same in the shoe or the computer store. But I want to emphasize what you just said. Yes, our relationship is mostly built around talking. We talk face to face and we phone and text and we email and we skype. All of these are about words and we try hard to use words that convey love and care and fun and that makes all the difference. It really matters a lot. Our words matter. They really do!"

Chapter 62

Sexuality

Romantic love is always accompanied by intense sexual desire. Both partners become ravenous for the other and their lovemaking is often more passionate, ecstatic and intimate than any previous sexual encounter. This new and exciting level of passion is one of the wonderful gifts of romantic love and, if properly nurtured, can be sustained and even increase in intensity for years or longer.

The sexual passion of romantic love lowers personal boundaries and invites an increasing deepening of intimacy. Sex and intimacy become partners in the couple's lovemaking and each contributes to the other. The power of lust mixed with the even greater power of romantic love drives both lovers to drop all pretenses and strip away, not only all their physical clothing but also all emotional and spiritual defenses. Romantic passion demands nakedness on all levels and each lover learns to revel in the freedom it offers.

Romantic passion also demands exploration. Each lover wants desperately to explore the body and the heart of the other as if it is a wondrous, unknown and mysterious territory. Just as each wants to know the other in preciously intimate detail, each lover also aches to be touched and heard and seen and felt by this one who has become the most desirable being in all existence.

Sexual encounter in the context of romantic love can thus be a doorway or a path to radical intimacy. It provides a physical and emotional intensity that overcomes the rigid defenses that usually block access to each partner's inner being. When these defenses drop in the midst of lovemaking, lovers can enter their partner's holiest inner sanctum and know and be known at a depth that is completely unavailable to any other person. This creates a sacred connection and an almost indescribable experience of loving, healing ecstasy and bliss.

Most romantically involved couples approach the doorway to this deeper connection. They glimpse what is beyond and then one or both turn away. They know that something more awaits, something that could be incredibly wonderful and life changing. But they stop, turn away and settle. This settling leads then to sameness and that sameness leads to a lessening of intimacy and intensity. Eventually their lovemaking becomes simply sex and too often a form of mutual masturbation bereft of romance.

Romantic love and its passionate sexuality do not have to come to this sad end. It can be sustained and it can deepen and expand. If both partners, both lovers, are willing to pass through the doorway described above. It takes courage, certain learnable skills, maturity and commitment and a willingness to surrender to love, of course, but the treasure to be found is greater than words can describe. Romantic love always opens the door and invites every lover to enter. It is up to us what happens next.

Chapter 63

Dianna and Michael – Sexuality

Michael volunteers to go first on this subject.

"Sex is a really important part of romantic love and our sexual relationship has proved that to be true. We came to each other with sexual experience. Neither of us was a virgin and we acknowledged that at the start. We did not discuss any former sexual partners in detail because we both agreed that would create problems. Couples who share details almost always end up comparing and competing with the past and that harms the connection in the present. I don't want to know who Dianna has been with and what it was like for her and she has the same attitude about me and my past. We have honored that decision to let the past be the past and we are both happy we did and do.

199

"OK, enough with the boring part. Let's talk about romantic sex or making love as we usually call it. Simply put, it is incredible! Romantic lovemaking is as different from usual sex as a ham sandwich is from a gourmet meal. No, that image does not do it justice. Let me try again. Romantic lovemaking is as different from usual sex as a rock is from a diamond. That is a much better image. I have had some rocks in my time, some more interesting than others, but not one was a diamond and the diamond I am referring to is not a one carat beginner's stone. It is massive and priceless.

"When we make love, whether it takes thirty minutes or two hours, giant walls come crashing down, explosions occur, our hearts touch and enter one another and the tenderness is almost excruciating. Love and lust lose their boundaries and flow between and within us so powerfully that we weep and sigh and hold each other so tightly that breathing becomes difficult. We are carried by rushing waves of emotion and desire that demand our surrender and we fall into each other's arms and legs and breasts and necks and hair as if each part was the first and most sacred we had ever encountered. Suddenly, in the midst of a ravenous moment, we pause and hold one another's face and look directly into each other's soul, past the eyes and deep into a place that only a fully surrendered lover can see. Precious tears flow and we often sob and do our best not to break the connection and lose that holy moment, and then we are carried away by a wave of lust and we dive back into a special sensuality that only those deeply in love can experience."

Dianna takes Michael's hand and picks up the conversation.

"Michael, I love your passion when you speak about these things almost as much as I do when we are in bed. (She laughs.) Everything you have described is true. That is what happens. It is beyond anything I ever knew or expected. In a sense, I think we are both virgins when it comes to this sort of love. I know we both have had sex with other people and sometimes we both thought it was pretty good but this, this is like the diamond you talked about before. When we are naked and you hold me and we look into each other's eyes, I feel completely innocent. I don't mean naïve, I mean pure, undefiled, new and virginal. In that moment we are both that way and every touch and kiss and sound has a fresh intensity as if we have never been with anyone else. I feel wonderfully overwhelmed by that feeling sometimes. It actually feels like a different kind of orgasm, one that is emotional and spiritual. I know you know what I mean. You have the same experience."

Michael laughs a hearty laugh and responds.

"Sweetheart, you said that so beautifully and accurately. Yes, that is what it is like and it is far more than the mutual masturbation sex that so many couples have. That is a way of getting off but what you are talking about is like discovering your own diamond mine. To call it wonderful is almost too trite. It is astounding. It shakes me to the core. I could go on and on about this but I want to add something if I may.

"I am convinced that this sort of lovemaking does something very special and important to both of us. It brings us to a level of trust and openness that affects us in every other area of our life together. It affects our relationship in a thousand ways and they are all good. These loving and passionate encounters break down our barriers and allow us to see and feel and trust each other beyond anything I have ever known. Sweetheart, when we make love that way I want to share all that I am with you. I feel so safe and so happily naked and I want to know you the same way. God, it is so exciting and healing and peaceful all at the same time."

Dianna jumps up from her chair, falls into Michael's lap and kisses his face. He begins to cry and puts his face in her neck.

Time to go.

Last Word

As you and your lover journey together on this magnificent path of romantic love, remember that you have been given a precious gift. Treasure it and each other. Let nothing except love come between you, and love will bless you both.

In Love.

Matthew

Note to Reader: To receive my free How to Be a World Class Romantic Lover: For Men and Women please email me at DrA@ Mattcoyote.com and put "World Class Lover" in the subject line.

*#1 INTERNATIONAL
BEST-SELLING BOOK*
in three categories:

*Love & Romance, Marriage,
Healthy Relationships*

Matthew Anderson, D.Min., has been a Coach-for-Life and motivational
speaker for over 40 years. He has authored three books and a variety
of CDs on relationships, love, inner work and spirituality.
He is also a nature photographer and a business coach.
He lives and works in Boca Raton, Florida.

- Blog about romantic love and relationships with Matthew
  at www.TheResurrectionofRomance.com

- Contact Matthew for couples and singles relationship coaching
  DrA@Mattcoyote.com or 561.362.4049

- Contact Matthew for speaking engagements
  at DrA@Mattcoyote.com

- For more CDs and relationship resources go to
  www.TheResurrectionofRomance.com

- To book Dianna and Michael for speaking engagements and
  couples workshops please email them at DrA@Mattcoyote.com